QM Library

KU-370-340

HM22.G32.H3 TWO

HABERMAS:
A GUIDE FOR THE PERPLEXED

Continuum Guides for the Perplexed

Continuum's Guides for the Perplexed are clear, concise and accessible introductions to thinkers, writers and subjects that students and readers can find especially challenging. Concentrating specifically on what it is that makes the subject difficult to grasp, these books explain and explore key themes and ideas, guiding the reader towards a thorough understanding of demanding material.

Guides for the Perplexed available from Continuum:

Adorno: A Guide for the Perplexed, Alex Thomson
Arendt: A Guide for the Perplexed, Karin Fry
Aristotle: A Guide for the Perplexed, John Vella
Bentham: A Guide for the Perplexed, Philip Schofield
Berkley: A Guide for the Perplexed, Talia Bettcher
Deleuze: A Guide for the Perplexed, Claire Colebrook
Derrida: A Guide for the Perplexed, Julian Wolfreys
Descartes: A Guide for the Perplexed, Justin Skirry
The Empiricists: A Guide for the Perplexed, Laurence Carlin
Existentialism: A Guide for the Perplexed, Stephen Earnshaw
Freud: A Guide for the Perplexed, Celine Surprenant
Gadamer: A Guide for the Perplexed, Chris Lawn
Hegel: A Guide for the Perplexed, David James
Heidegger: A Guide for the Perplexed, David Cerbone
Hobbes: A Guide for the Perplexed, Stephen J. Finn
Hume: A Guide for the Perplexed, Angela Coventry
Husserl: A Guide for the Perplexed, Matheson Russell
Kant: A Guide for the Perplexed, T. K. Seung
Kierkegaard: A Guide for the Perplexed, Clare Carlisle
Leibniz: A Guide for the Perplexed, Franklin Perkins
Levinas: A Guide for the Perplexed, B. C. Hutchens
Merleau-Ponty: A Guide for the Perplexed, Eric Matthews
Nietzsche: A Guide for the Perplexed, R. Kevin Hill
Plato: A Guide for the Perplexed, Gerald A. Press
Pragmatism: A Guide for the Perplexed, Robert B. Talisse and Scott F. Aikin
Quine: A Guide for the Perplexed, Gary Kemp
Relativism: A Guide for the Perplexed, Timothy Mosteller
Ricoeur: A Guide for the Perplexed, David Pellauer
Rousseau: A Guide for the Perplexed, Matthew Simpson
Sartre: A Guide for the Perplexed, Gary Cox
Socrates: A Guide for the Perplexed, Sara Ahbel-Rappe
Spinoza: A Guide for the Perplexed, Charles Jarrett
The Stoics: A Guide for the Perplexed, M. Andrew Holowchak
Utilitarianism: A Guide for the Perplexed: Krister Bykvist

HABERMAS:
A GUIDE FOR THE PERPLEXED

LASSE THOMASSEN

continuum

Continuum International Publishing Group

The Tower Building   80 Maiden Lane
11 York Road   Suite 704
London SE1 7NX   New York, NY 10038

www.continuumbooks.com

© Lasse Thomassen 2010

All rights reserved. No part of this publication may be reproduced or
transmitted in any form or by any means, electronic or mechanical,
including photocopying, recording, or any information storage or retrieval
system, without prior permission in writing from the publishers.

British Library Cataloguing-in-Publication Data
A catalogue record for this book is available from the British Library.

ISBN: HB: 978-0-8264-8765-0
PB: 978-0-8264-8766-7

Library of Congress Cataloging-in-Publication Data
Thomassen, Lasse.
Habermas : a guide for the perplexed / Lasse Thomassen.
p. cm.
Includes bibliographical references and index.
ISBN-13: 978-0-8264-8765-0 (HB)
ISBN-10: 0-8264-8765-3 (HB)
ISBN-13: 978-0-8264-8766-7 (pbk.)
ISBN-10: 0-8264-8766-1 (pbk.)
1. Habermas, Jürgen. I. Title.
B3258.H324T46 2010
193–dc22
2009022134

QM LIBRARY
(MILE END)

Typeset by Newgen Imaging Systems Pvt Ltd, Chennai, India
Printed and bound in Great Britain by CPI Antony Rowe,
Chippenham, Wiltshire

For Beatriz

CONTENTS

ACKNOWLEDGEMENTS

Thanks to Beatriz Martínez Fernández, Ian O'Flynn and Marina Prentoulis who read and commented on parts of the book. Thanks also to Tom Crick and Sarah Campbell at Continuum for their continuing support in the process of writing the book and for steering me carefully through the whole process. I dedicate this book to Beatriz who tolerated my mental and physical absences while writing it. Of course, I cannot promise that there will be no more such absences in the future.

INTRODUCTION

THE PERPLEXITY OF HABERMAS

Jürgen Habermas is difficult to read and often leaves students perplexed. There are three mutually related reasons for this. One reason is that Habermas was trained as a philosopher in the best German tradition, and so he writes as someone who knows the philosophical tradition and who expects his readers to do the same. Apart from philosophy, Habermas draws on sociology, political theory, psychology and other disciplines. The vocabularies and assumptions of these disciplines often make their way into Habermas's own work, thus making it more difficult to read.

Habermas is also difficult to read because he writes in an abstract and conceptual – we might say 'philosophical' – style. Among other things, this is due to the fact that Habermas is engaged in grand theorizing, for which he makes use of abstract and conceptual arguments. His theories are theories about society, language, law and democracy, rather than theories about this or that particular social phenomenon.

Finally, Habermas is difficult to read because of the language he writes in. He uses long sentences, packed with theoretical concepts, and so his style is difficult to comprehend for first-time readers. His style is systematic though, and usually his books are well translated from the German. This is especially the case with his later works.

Making sense of Habermas

To illustrate the difficulties in reading and understanding Habermas, take the following quote from Habermas's (1996a, xlii) most important work in the area of political philosophy, *Between Facts and Norms*:

> In the final analysis, private legal subjects cannot come to enjoy equal individual liberties if they do not *themselves*, in the common exercise of their political autonomy, achieve clarity about justified interests and standards. They themselves must agree on the relevant aspects under which equals should be treated equally and unequals unequally.

Although it is taken out of context, first-time – and even second-time – readers are excused for feeling perplexed at reading sentences like these. The quote is from the Preface to *Between Facts and Norms*, and Habermas is trying to explain the main point of the book ('in the final analysis').

The book is about law and democracy, and specifically about what makes law legitimate. That is, the book concerns this question: when can we follow the law out of respect for the law rather than just following it because we fear the reprisals if we break the law? The book – and the quote – speaks to long-standing debates in philosophy and in legal and political theory about equality and freedom. When can we say about citizens that they are free and enjoy this freedom equally? What does it mean to be free? And so on. These are questions addressed by philosophers such as Jean-Jacques Rousseau and Immanuel Kant and, today, in the debate between liberals and republicans. If we know this background, the quote makes much better sense.

The quote also exhibits Habermas's abstract style of writing. He uses concepts such as 'legal subject' and 'political autonomy'. Only if we are already well versed in the terminology of legal and political theory will these concepts function as planks we can hold onto. The abstract nature of Habermas's writings, including this quote, can also be attributed to his aim, namely to devise a theory of law and democracy in general. Finally, Habermas's use of long and complex sentences – littered with theoretical concepts – is easily visible in the quote.

Any explication and explanation of Habermas's work will add to, but also take away from, the meaning of Habermas's own words. That applies to this book as well. Any explication and explanation is a bit like a translation; in this book, I will try to translate Habermas's language into a more easily accessible language. Things will inevitably get lost, but hopefully this will not outweigh the gain in understanding.

Here, for example, is a translation of the quote above from *Between Facts and Norms*. Habermas here says that the bottom line of his theory of law and democracy is that freedom has two sides. There is freedom from the interference from others (also called negative freedom); this is often expressed as individual rights to free speech, and so on. More generally, the law is what gives me my status as a citizen, including the rights that come with this status. But to be free, I must be able to see myself as not just subject to the law, but also as author of the law (this is what Habermas means by 'political autonomy' here). The underlying idea is autonomy, literally self-legislation (auto-nomy). We should give ourselves our own laws, which should not be imposed upon us by the rulers. If we have autonomy, then we have legitimate law; we will act in accordance with the law out of respect for it because we have authored – and authorized – the law ourselves. The law decides how to treat different citizens, sometimes equally (giving them identical rights), sometimes unequally (different rights). In the case of parental leave, for instance, the law may reflect relevant differences between women/mothers and men/fathers. Given the underlying value of autonomy, citizens themselves are the ones to decide what the relevant differences are. If citizens have given themselves their own laws, then we can say about them that they are free, and that they are free each in their way.

This book will try to make sense of Habermas. I will try to make up for the difficulties in reading and understanding Habermas by translating Habermas into a more accessible language and give a systematic account of the main tenets of his work. Although I shall mention some of the criticisms that have been raised against Habermas, the aim of the book is not to find contradictions or oversights in Habermas's work; rather, this introduction is meant as a friendly reconstruction of Habermas's work.

To make better sense of Habermas's writings, I place them against their relevant backgrounds: the philosophical debates and the political contexts into which he intervenes. I shall also explain key concepts and passages in detail. To shed light on more theoretical points, I use his political interventions. For instance, in Chapter 5 on Habermas's theory of law and democracy, I use his writings on civil disobedience in Germany in the 1980s to explain how Habermas thinks about the legitimacy of the law. Finally, I make links between different parts of Habermas's work and make comparisons with other thinkers so that the similarities and contrasts with other thinkers cast light on Habermas's own position.

Those readers who want to read more will find ample references to Habermas's own works as well as to further introductions and discussions of his work throughout the book, especially in the 'Further Readings' sections at the end of each chapter and in the bibliography. Hopefully this book is only the first step in reading (about) Habermas.

LIFE AND WORK

Martin Heidegger once said about Aristotle that all we need to know about Aristotle's life for understanding his philosophy was that he was born, worked and died. In short, it is not necessary to know anything about Aristotle's life in order to understand his philosophy. Jürgen Habermas was born in 1929, he has written a number of books, most important of which are *The Theory of Communicative Action* (1984; 1987a) and *Between Facts and Norms* (1996a).

It would be a mistake to end the introduction to Habermas's life there, however, even if it is a common mistake. In academia, we usually make a distinction between the work and the person and look at the work in isolation from the life of the author. Often philosophy, theory and science are seen as literally disembodied: what matters are the thoughts, the insights and the truths, less who arrived at them and in what context. If they are true, ideas are supposedly universal and ahistorical. So we read books and articles by philosophers and about philosophical issues, but we do not usually study the sex-lives of philosophers. Similarly with Habermas. Very few introductions go beyond a brief sketch of Habermas's life, and Habermas himself only briefly touches upon his autobiography in interviews.[1]

Although I shall not make a great deal of Habermas's biography, one of the assumptions of this book is that biography matters. This is so first of all for pedagogical reasons: it is easier to make sense of Habermas's work if we relate it to his life and to the philosophical and political context in which he is writing. But there is a more principled reason for highlighting Habermas's biography, namely that nothing is not influenced by its context. Habermas's work must be understood against different background contexts: philosophical debates, political debates in Germany since World War II – and his life story. Thus, I shall introduce some biographical information in this brief introduction to his life and work, and I will refer to it in later chapters when relevant.

It is important not to reduce Habermas's work to his biography though. I do not want to give the impression that we can explain what Habermas writes simply by pointing to the personal, philosophical and political contexts of his writings. This would suggest a strong causal determination of the work by the context, as if the work was already written before Habermas had set pen to paper. Rather, making sense of Habermas's work by putting it into context is always retrospective and proceeds in the clear light of hindsight. Any context is an open context. It presents certain possibilities to us as agents, and – according to how we interpret them – we pursue some of these rather than others, and in turn we influence the context.

What are, then, the facts about Habermas? He was born in 1929 and grew up in the small town of Gummersbach near Cologne. He grew up in a bourgeois, middle-class family, and he characterizes the political climate at home as 'a middle class conformity to a political environment with which one did not completely identify, but which one also did not criticize' (in Horster and van Reijen 1992, 77). His childhood and adolescence were relatively sheltered from the events during Nazism and World War II. Like other children of his age, Habermas joined the Hitler Jugend towards the end of the war, and he was sent to help at the western line of defence.

Habermas was born with a cleft palate ('hare lip'), which makes him difficult to understand when he speaks. In a recent essay, he addresses this for the first time. At home, his family could understand him, but he had difficulties when going to school. In the essay, Habermas (2008, 15) writes that this childhood experience could have inspired his communicative approach to society and morality: 'Failures of communication direct our attention to an otherwise unobtrusive intermediary world of symbols that cannot be grasped like physical objects' (ibid.). The thesis is that Habermas's problem with communicating has led him to consider what he calls 'the power of language to forge a community' (ibid.). For Habermas, language and communication take centre stage, and he arrives at his theories of discourse ethics and deliberative democracy through a theory of language and communication. One way to express this is to say that language and communication define us as human beings. We are *homo communicatus*, and this – rather than *homo economicus* or *laborans* – is what distinguishes us as human beings.

Habermas mentions another related childhood experience: an operation he had immediately after being born. He writes that this experience 'may well have awakened the feelings of dependence and vulnerability and the sense of the relevance of our interactions *with others*' (ibid., 13). I am not interested in whether or not this was really the case. Rather, what is interesting is the link Habermas makes between this and what is a leitmotif of his work: every individual is a social being. We are born into a social environment, we become what we are through social exchanges, and so on. In short, we are *homo socius*. In Habermas's work, this is expressed in the emphasis on intersubjectivity. What is important is what happens among subjects – hence also the emphasis on language and communication.

So much for Habermas's childhood. After the fall of Nazi Germany in 1945, Habermas realized the horrors of Nazism and the Holocaust. He says:

> [I]t was the events of the year 1945 that set my political motives. At that time my personal life rhythm and the great historical events of the time coincided. There were reports on the radio about the Nuremberg trials, and in the movie theaters they showed the first documentary films, the films about the concentration camps that we are seeing again today. I am sure that out of these experiences, motivations developed that determined the further course of my thinking. (in Horster and van Reijen 1992, 77f.)

For Habermas, defeat became liberation. He came to see liberal democracy – as found in France or the United States – as an achievement in itself. In this, he distinguished himself from those who associated liberal democracy with the instability and frailty of the Weimar Republic. It also distinguished him from a later generation that came of age in the 1960s and took liberal democracy to be merely the mask of capitalist exploitation.

However, the immediate post-World War II period also brought disappointments for Habermas. On the political front, the disappointment was the lack of a clear break with the Nazi past. This was evident, for instance, in the continuity in the elites in the universities, in politics and in many other areas of German society.

During those years, Habermas studied philosophy first at Göttingen, then at Zurich and finally at Bonn. He read German philosophy, but also the neo-Marxist Georg Lukács and the early Karl Marx. In 1954, he finished his PhD thesis on the philosophy of the German idealist Friedrich Schelling. During these years, Habermas was also a vivid reader of Heidegger. However, here too he became disappointed.

The disappointment was not with Heidegger's philosophy, but with the fact that Heidegger was silent about his collaboration with the Nazis. The disappointment was not that Heidegger had been wrong, but that he would not own up to his mistake. Heidegger became rector of the University of Freiburg after the Nazis took power in 1933, he joined the Nazi party and in some of his writings he linked his philosophy to central ideas in Nazism. After the war, Heidegger did what many other Germans did too: nothing. He simply kept quiet. Although Habermas still thinks of Heidegger as one of the most important philosophers of the twentieth century, Heidegger's silence gave birth to a suspicion about Heidegger's philosophy. Habermas's disappointment with Heidegger let him to recognize the interdependence between an author's philosophy and his or her politics. In Heidegger's philosophy, Habermas found a basis for Heidegger's political support for Nazism. Since then, Habermas has insisted that philosophy is always also political and must be so. Ideally, philosophy should be critical and should support an emancipatory politics. Later, Habermas charged post-structuralists such as Michel Foucault and Jacques Derrida with leaving the door open for conservative forces because their approaches allegedly lacked critical foundations (Habermas 1987c; see also Kelly 1994; Thomassen 2006).

During the 1950s, Habermas became interested in political culture and the role of the media, among other things as a result of his disappointments with German political culture after Nazism and the Holocaust. After finishing his PhD in 1954, Habermas worked as a journalist. From 1956 to 1959, he worked as a research assistant for the philosopher and sociologist Theodor Adorno at the Institute for Social Research at Frankfurt University. Together with Max Horkheimer, Adorno was one of the founders of the Institute in the 1920s. They belong to the first generation of what later became known as the Frankfurt School. Habermas would eventually become identified as the second generation of Frankfurt School theorists.

As Jews and leftists, Adorno and Horkheimer fled Germany in 1933 when the Nazis took power, but they returned to Frankfurt after the war and became influential in German intellectual life. In Frankfurt, Habermas was exposed to sociological theory (Max Weber, Émile Durkheim, and others) as well as earlier Critical Theorists such as Ernst Bloch, Herbert Marcuse and Walter Benjamin. However, Adorno did not accept Habermas's habilitation thesis, so Habermas moved to Marburg University to work with the historian Wolfgang Abendroth. At this time, Habermas was involved in two book projects, both of which examined political culture and the state of the public sphere in Germany.

First, together with other researchers, he examined the political culture of students in German universities (Habermas et al. 1961). Later, towards the end of the 1960s, Habermas became embroiled in debates about the 1967–68 student protests.

Second, in 1962, Habermas published his habilitation thesis *The Structural Transformation of the Public Sphere* (1989a), which I shall return to in Chapter 2. The book became immensely influential in Germany and beyond. Habermas argued that a public sphere emerged from the coffee houses in Paris and London in the 1800s. Although the ideal of a power-free public sphere never really materialized, the ideal was there nonetheless. What gained most tract, however, was Habermas's diagnosis of the contemporary German public sphere. He argued that the public sphere was increasingly dominated by vested monetary interests that reduce politics to a mass democracy where citizens are passive spectators rather than active participants.

In 1962, Habermas took up a position at Heidelberg University, and in 1964 he returned to Frankfurt to succeed Horkheimer as professor of philosophy and sociology. From then on, Habermas would become synonym with the Frankfurt School of Critical Theory.

During his years at Frankfurt until 1971, Habermas engaged in philosophical debates about the status of critical theory and social science. He criticized both positivists like Karl Popper and hermeneuticists like Hans-Georg Gadamer. For Habermas, both positivism and hermeneutics are incapable of supporting a social science that is critical of contemporary society and can point a way towards an emancipated society. The fruits of this work were published in two books in particular, *Theory and Practice* (1988a) and *Knowledge and Human Interests* (1987b).

Parallel to this philosophical work, Habermas engaged himself with the student movement in Germany. His writings – including *The Structural Transformation of the Public Sphere* (1989a) – inspired the students, and he spoke out on their behalf. However, it came to a sort of break in 1967. While Habermas supported the students' demands for radical reforms of society and of the universities, he was wary of their tactics. Like the students, Habermas was critical of the political elites, including the Social Democrats, but he thought it premature to declare the students to be the new proletariat and, as such, the new revolutionary class. Instead, he argued, the students had to work on public opinion in order to create alliances with other groups in society, including workers. He criticized the students for what he called their 'actionism'. His point was that action for the sake of action (happenings, and so on) are not particularly effective in changing public opinion. Thus, Habermas's idea is that one must work through the public sphere to convince others and to create a more lasting change of political culture. Habermas eventually became vilified by the students as a defender of the system, and this image has to some extent stuck to him since. The student protests died out, however, although they did have a lasting impact on German culture and society (Habermas 1971, chapters 1–3; 1981, parts I–II).

From 1971 to 1982, Habermas took up a position as director at the Max Planck Institute in Starnberg outside Munich. It was during these years that Habermas developed his theory of language and, on this basis, his theory of communicative action and rationality.

In his inaugural speech at Frankfurt in 1965, Habermas had fore-shadowed this turn to language and communication. He wrote: 'What raises us out of nature is the only thing whose nature we can know: *language*. Through its structure, autonomy and responsibility are posited for us. Our first sentence expresses unequivocally the intention of universal and unconstrained consensus' (Habermas 1987b, 314). I shall return to this quote in Chapter 1. Here I just want to draw attention to the constitutive nature of language. What distinguishes us as humans is our use of language. Looking at language and how we use language, Habermas finds that whenever we communicate, we implicitly assume that we can reach a universal and power-free consensus. This is the crux of his universal pragmatics that he developed in a number of writings during the 1970s (Habermas

1998a; 2001a). The idea is quite simply that if language is what defines us, then we must look to our use of language for an account of morality. Whenever we use language, so Habermas, we assume that, under idealized circumstances of the free exchange of reasons, it is possible to reach a universal, unconstrained consensus. Initially, Habermas referred to this as the 'ideal speech situation'. The outcome is a rational consensus, which we can use as a critical ideal against which to compare any de facto consensus. So, Habermas's critical theory starts from the analysis of language, and he finds a critical ideal in the way we use language.

At the end of this period, Habermas published the monumental – two volumes, 900 pages – *The Theory of Communicative Action* (1984; 1987a). In there, he developed a theory of communicative action and rationality. The basic theses are these. First, social action is more than instrumental and strategic action where I try to manipulate the world and other people in order to achieve an end. There is another kind of action which is action oriented towards mutual understanding; this he calls communicative action. Second, and linked to this, there is a kind of rationality that is not a means–ends rationality. This is communicative rationality, which is linked to achieving rational consensus through rational discourse. Rationality is linked to the public use of reason; it is the quality of that reason giving that determines the rationality of the outcome. The argument is much more complex, and I return to it in Chapter 3.

In the late 1970s, and after some years of relative silence, Habermas (1981) again intervened in political debates in Germany. This time the debates were about the terrorism of the *Rote Armee Fraktion* (*RAF*) and *Berufsverbot*, the ban on communists to occupy certain jobs such as public school teachers. In the 1980s, Habermas too engaged in public debates, this time about civil disobedience, American nuclear missiles on German soil (Habermas 1985), and later about German identity and history and the Holocaust. Common to these debates and to the debates about German reunification in 1989–90 is the question of how Germans should understand themselves and their history. Habermas (1989b; 1997) argued that the Holocaust and the break with Nazism must be central to German political identity. Here there is a clear link to Habermas's experiences in the post-war period.

Furthermore, he argued, German political identity must be just that: political. This became equally important in debates about immigration in the 1990s. What Habermas means is that a modern, pluralist society such as Germany cannot be held together by a substantive identity based on ethnicity, culture and so on (1997). Instead, society must be integrated through a common political culture. Habermas refers to 'constitutional patriotism' in this regard. In short, what should bind us together is allegiance to a common political culture expressed in the values and principles of the constitution (1996a, 500).

After *The Theory of Communicative Action*, Habermas developed the theory of communicative action and rationality into a theory of discourse ethics. Put simply, for Habermas, the question 'what is normatively right?' cannot be answered by the philosopher, but should be answered through discourses among real people. That is, people should debate under circumstances that are free from inequality, manipulation and so on. The result will be a rational consensus (Habermas 1990).

From the late 1980s onwards, Habermas started developing a theory of politics, law and democracy. This is not to suggest that he was not concerned with politics before, on the contrary. But with *Between Facts and Norms* (1996a), Habermas developed his discourse ethics into a theory of deliberative democracy, which is the subject of Chapter 5. The central idea of deliberative democracy is similar to that of discourse ethics. Those who are subject to (moral or legal) norms should be able to see themselves as also the authors of those norms. In short, we are dealing with autonomy as rational self-legislation. The rationality comes from the fact that decisions are reached through deliberations (or discourses) that are free from domination. Given the emphasis on deliberation, the public sphere is absolutely central. Here we find again the red thread running through Habermas's writings – the public use of reason – from the public sphere through communicative action and rationality to discourse ethics and then, finally, to deliberative democracy.

In 1994, Habermas retired from Frankfurt, although he remains professor emeritus there. He has by no means stopped working though. He gives numerous lectures around the world every year, and he also continues to publish. He has intervened in public debates about the European Union, 9-11 and the so-called war on terror, Iraq and the new world order, and many other issues (Habermas 2003b; 2006a–b; 2009). For over fifty years, Habermas has been the incarnation of a public intellectual.

His other recent writings have focused on philosophical issues surrounding the status of his theories, but he has also focused attention on more concrete issues. Among the latter is the role of religion in contemporary Western societies (2008, parts II and III). This includes an exchange with Joseph Ratzinger, now Pope Benedict XVI (Habermas and Ratzinger 2005). Finally, Habermas has been involved in debates about new gene technologies and human nature, and the implications of these for the autonomy of persons (Habermas 2003b). In Chapter 6, I summarize Habermas's positions on these issues.

Habermas's work spans more than five decades and, for the moment, it shows no sign of abating. If there is one red thread running through it, then it is the idea of the public use of reason, that is, the idea that both philosophy and society are better off relying on the forceless force of the better argument. We find the idea of the public use of reason in Habermas's work on the public sphere, in his theories of language and communication, including the theory of communicative action and rationality, in his discourse ethics and in his theory of deliberative democracy. Whether the emphasis on intersubjectivity, communication and political culture can be traced back to Habermas's experiences as a child and adolescent remains an open question. What remains, however, is a thinker who draws upon a wide variety of sources from a variety of disciplines, brings them together in a theory of language and society, in constant dialogue with other thinkers and with developments in society, and brings them to bear on concrete contemporary issues.

THE STRUCTURE OF THE BOOK

This book covers the most important topics in Habermas's work, and the most important aspects of those topics.

Chapter 1 situates Habermas in relation to other critical theorists. Habermas belongs to the second generation of the so-called Frankfurt School of Critical Theory, and I compare and contrast his work to that of the first generation, especially Adorno and Horkheimer. I explain what Habermas takes on board from them, but also what he criticizes in them and how he tries to move beyond the Critical theory of the earlier Frankfurt School. I introduce Habermas's idea of a critical theory of society, its aims and reach, and I explain his critique of scientism and hermeneutics. Central to Habermas's proposal for a critical theory is a turn to what he calls an intersubjectivist philosophy, that is, one that takes language and communication as its starting points.

In Chapter 2, I introduce Habermas's writings on the public sphere, especially his seminal *The Structural Transformation of the Public Sphere* (1989a), which was first published in 1962. I also look at criticisms of this book as well as Habermas's partial reformulation of the earlier argument. Anticipating subsequent chapters, I explain the idea of the public use of reason, and how Habermas believes that this will solve a number of problems central to philosophy, morality, politics and law. The emphasis on the public use of reason is linked to the emphasis on language and communication and, later, to the reformulation of autonomy in terms of deliberative democracy.

The Theory of Communicative Action (1984; 1987a) is the focus of Chapter 3. I explain the main ideas of that work and how Habermas arrived at them. In particular, I focus on the notions of communicative action and rationality, and how these are grounded in a theory of the formal pragmatics of language. Also important is the way Habermas links a critical theory of society to language and communication through the account of communicative action and rationality. The critical upshot of *The Theory of Communicative Action* is a distinction between systems and lifeworld and the so-called colonization thesis. The idea is that systems such as the state and the market 'colonize' areas that are not usually integrated through power and money, and this has alienating effects in society. This is Habermas's attempt to update Critical Theory with a more contemporary critique of the bureaucratization and marketization of society.

On the basis of his theory of communicative rationality, Habermas proposed a discourse ethics (or rather, a discourse theory of validity). This is the subject of Chapter 4, which explains Habermas's theory of validity, including the validity of social norms. Habermas understands validity as discursive. What is normatively right is what people arrive at in discourses that are free from inequality, domination, etc., and where only the forceless force of the better argument rules. Habermas argues that it is possible to talk about a kind of objectivity in normative matters, and here he distinguishes himself from, among others, so-called post-modernists. He also argues against teleology and believes that his discourse ethics is a deontological theory where the right enjoys primacy over the good. In this, he distinguishes himself from communitarians who posit the good of the community as a whole as prior to the rights of individuals.

Habermas always engaged in political debates, and he was always attuned to the political implications of his philosophy. Only from the mid-1980s does he address political institutions head-on, however. He does so with a notion of discursive democracy that he refers to as a theory of deliberative democracy and law, which he develops in *Between Facts and Norms* (1996a). There he translates his discourse theory of validity into a theory of deliberative democracy. This is the focus of Chapter 5. The central idea is that law is legitimate insofar as the addressees of the law can see themselves as also the authors of the law. Thus, the central idea is autonomy, or self-legislation, but it must be rational, and this is where deliberation enters into the picture. If everybody possibly affected by a law have had the opportunity to have a say in the deliberations leading up to the law, then we can talk about deliberative autonomy. Rationality and legitimacy are located in communication and discourse, and so in this chapter I return to the public use of reason, which runs like a red thread through Habermas's work.

Chapter 6 examines three issues that have been the focus of Habermas's work since the mid-1990s. The first issue concerns the nation-state. Habermas argues that we must develop supra-national democratic institutions, both at European and world level. The second issue is the role of religion in contemporary societies. Habermas has written about tolerance, secularism and religion, and he argues for what he calls 'post-secularism' where religion is taken seriously as an equal partner in dialogue with reason. The third, and final, issue concerns the challenges raised by new gene technologies to our conception of what it means to be an autonomous human being. Thus, Chapter 6 shows how Habermas puts his theories of communicative action, discourse ethics and deliberative democracy to work on these more specific issues of contemporary relevance.

FURTHER READINGS

Martin Matuštík's (2001) *Jürgen Habermas: A Philosophical–Political Profile* places Habermas's philosophy and politics in the context of German culture and society. The interviews in *Autonomy and Solidarity*, edited by Peter Dews, offer a useful introduction to Habermas's work and the way he links his work to contemporary events. Habermas's autobiographical essay (2008, chapter 1) is an interesting, retrospective view on his life and work.

CHAPTER ONE

TOWARDS A CRITICAL THEORY OF SOCIETY

INTRODUCTION

Where do you begin? Where do you begin an introduction to someone like Habermas who has written so much and across so many fields? One could present Habermas's work chronologically, starting with his first publication; one could begin in one corner or begin with an overview; and so on. Wherever one begins, the end result must be coherent or at least as coherent as the work one is introducing; and, given that it is impossible to cover everything, the end result must emphasize the most relevant points. Whether the work is in fact coherent, and what the most relevant points are – these are of course often open questions.

I begin by placing Habermas within what is generally referred to as Critical Theory. One of the specific aims of this chapter is, thus, to place Habermas within an intellectual tradition, namely that of Critical Theory going back to Karl Marx through Max Horkheimer and Theodor Adorno. This is not to say that Habermas is only, or even primarily, a Critical Theorist, although he is also that, and he is often identified as an important representative of Critical Theory. I shall explain what Habermas takes from Marx, Horkheimer and Adorno and what he criticizes about them. This is the subject of the first two sections.

In the subsequent two sections, I explain how Habermas develops an alternative Critical Theory, first through the notion of 'human interests' and later through a turn to language and communication. The latter inaugurates what I believe to be the red thread running through Habermas's work, namely the public use of reason. It is in the public use of reason that Habermas finds a critical ideal, an ideal that is not realized in contemporary society but is nonetheless imma-nent to many of our institutions and everyday practices. The latter can then be measured and criticized against the critical ideal. In sub-sequent chapters, I follow this red thread in other areas of Habermas's work. Thus, I begin this introduction to Habermas by introducing what emerges as the red thread that gives coherence to his thinking, namely the public use of reason. I do this, in this chapter, in relation to Habermas as a Critical Theorist, explaining how Habermas comes to refashion Critical Theory around language, communication and the public use of reason.

WHAT IS CRITICAL THEORY?

Habermas belongs to the second generation of the so-called Frankfurt School (Bottomore 2002; Jay 1973). The latter is in turn often taken to be identical to Critical Theory *tout court*, although strictly speak-ing Critical Theory comprises more than just the Frankfurt School. Nevertheless, it is useful to place Habermas in relation to the Frankfurt School and in particular its most prominent earlier members, Max Horkheimer and Theodor Adorno.

The Frankfurt School is called so because its members belong or belonged to the Institute for Social Research which was established at Frankfurt University in 1924.[1] The first generation of Frankfurt School theorists included Horkheimer and Adorno as well as people like Friedrich Pollock and Herbert Marcuse. Apart from being socialists, some of the members of the Institute were Jewish, and so they fled Germany during the 1930s. Several of them – including Horkheimer and Adorno – ended up in the United States, where they established the Institute in New York City. After the end of World War II, Horkheimer and Adorno relocated the Institute to Frankfurt. Habermas first worked at the Institute from 1956 to 1959 as a research assistant for Adorno, and he returned in 1964. Apart from the years 1971 to 1982, he remained at the Institute and shaped the research undertaken there until his retirement in 1994. Where Horkheimer and Adorno belong to the first generation of Frankfurt School theo-rists, Habermas belongs to the second generation and the current director of the Institute and student of Habermas, Axel Honneth, is said to belong to a third generation of Frankfurt School critical theorists (Pensky 1998).

Before turning to Horkheimer's definition of Critical Theory, I will present Axel Honneth's (2001; see also 1999) research programme at the Institute for Social Research for the years 2001–2004: 'Paradoxes of Capitalist Modernization: The Foundations of a Comprehensive Research Project of the Institute for Social Research'. Despite the differences between the earlier Frankfurt School theory of Horkheimer and Adorno and the later theories of Habermas and Honneth, the latter's research programme expresses very well the general thrust of the critical theory of the Frankfurt School. For the purposes of this introduction, the programme can be summed up in five main points.

The research programme is, first, aimed at an analysis of contemporary, late capitalist society. More generally, Critical Theorists engage with contemporary issues. Habermas, for instance, has addressed different political and social issues throughout his career, both in his theoretical works and in his occasional pieces. Thus, today, he is interested in the role of religion in secularist societies and in the moral implications of new biotechnologies (cf. also Chapter 6).

Second, Honneth's research programme focuses on different areas of society, including ones that may seem trivial: the workplace, family, culture, the welfare state and so on. This is a general trait of the critical theory of the Frankfurt School. The reason for the focus on a range of areas is that inequality and alienation occur in all areas of society, not just within the state or the traditional economic sphere. Still, Honneth characterizes contemporary society as capitalist, thus reflecting the Marxist heritage of the Frankfurt School. Both the first generation of Frankfurt School theorists and Habermas broke with Marxism in important ways, however, and none of the Frankfurt School theorists would reduce social analysis and critique to the analysis of capitalism.

Third, given the focus on many different aspects of society, it is not surprising that Honneth's research programme for the Institute is also interdisciplinary. Like the work of other Frankfurt School theorists, the research programme draws on insights from a range of disciplines: political science, law, sociology, cultural studies and philosophy. This reflects their view of society as a totality where inequality and alienation in one part spills over into other parts. Capitalist production, for instance, becomes the paradigm for culture and so Horkheimer and Adorno talk about the 'culture industry' (Horkheimer and Adorno 2002). In Habermas's (1989a) book on the public sphere and modern media, he argues that, by the early 1960s, ideas and reasons had become reduced to commodities. Like Honneth, Horkheimer and Adorno as well as Habermas draw on a number of disciplines and on different theoretical sources, including German idealist philosophy, Marxism, Max Weber's theory of modern society and Freudian psychoanalysis.

Fourth, Honneth's research programme draws on both social sciences and philosophy. For Honneth and other Frankfurt School theorists, philosophy is an essential part of the critical analysis of society because philosophy provides normative inputs for that analysis. Equally, philosophical reflection on the scientific process is necessary, because the latter is informed by philosophical assumptions whether we admit to these or not. At the same time, philosophy must be linked to empirical studies in order for philosophical critique not to be empty. This combination of social science and philosophy is a general trait of the work of Frankfurt School theorists, including Habermas.

Fifth, and finally, Honneth's research programme refers to the 'paradoxes of capitalist modernisation'. This is a recurrent theme among theorists from the Frankfurt School: the ambiguity of progress. Honneth (2001) writes:

> One can speak of such paradoxical processes in relation to social developments whenever one and the same structural transformation brings about moral, legal and material progress through mechanisms that at the same time place these normative accomplishments in danger, because in the process the social prerequisites for taking advantage of them are eliminated or the meaning and purpose of these accomplishments are subverted.

It is obvious that modernity and capitalism have brought not just material progress, but also legal and moral progress, for instance the breakdown of old hierarchies through the rule of law. However, this progress comes hand in hand with developments that undermine the progress. For instance, we may be equals under law, but at the same time we are treated merely as legal subjects, and it may be argued that citizens become disempowered by the very welfare state provisions that were supposed to empower them (this is part of Habermas's so-called 'colonization thesis', to which I return in Chapter 3).

Horkheimer and Adorno articulated the ambiguity of progress in terms of the ambiguity of reason: rationalization, they argued, leads simultaneously to progress and to domination. Although Habermas and Honneth too are sensitive to the ambiguous nature of rationalization and of progress, they are more optimistic than Horkheimer and Adorno. Indeed, this points to a major difference between the first generation of Frankfurt School theorists and the second and third generations. Horkheimer and Adorno talk about the paradoxes and ambiguities of reason and modernity. They do so most famously in *Dialectic of Enlightenment* (2002), which was written during their years in exile in New York, and which offers a very bleak picture of modernity. There they argue that the essence of reason is control and domination, and that reason works on the principle of identity, thus rendering everything the same in a totalitarian fashion. Honneth, on the other hand, emphasizes a particular aspect of modernity, namely capitalism, and he associates the ambiguity of progress with this particular aspect of modernity. Analogously, Habermas argues that the problem is not reason as such, but one particular kind of reason, namely instrumental reason. Thus, his response to Horkheimer and Adorno is that we must differentiate reason, and that there is an emancipatory potential in the kind of reason that he calls communicative reason.

These five points about Honneth's research programme at the Institute for Social Research give a good idea of the kind of research that the Frankfurt School theorists – including Habermas – pursue. I will now turn to Horkheimer's (1986; see also 1993) influential definition of Critical Theory in an article from 1937. There Horkheimer makes a distinction between 'traditional' and 'critical' theory.

For what Horkheimer calls traditional theory, knowledge consists in information about the world and in subsuming nature and society to categories and concepts. Thus we have a subject (the scientist) who applies concepts to an object (the natural or social world). The aim is control and manipulation of nature and society, and so science and theory are measured according to their usefulness, according to an ideal of instrumental reason. Note that for the social sciences, society becomes an object, and Horkheimer is at pains to show that traditional theory works on a distinction between subject and object. The consequence is that social life becomes objectified because subjects are treated as objects. Science becomes isolated from its object and from the social context that made scientific enquiry possible in the first place. One of the main problems with traditional theory, according to Horkheimer, is that it is not self-reflective; it cannot reflect on its genesis or on how it is applied and on how its genesis and application are embedded within particular social contexts.

Horkheimer (1986, 213) writes:

> [T]he world which is given to the individual and which he must accept and take into account is, in its present and continuing form, a product of the activity of society as a whole. The objects we perceive in our surroundings – cities, villages, fields, and woods – bear the mark of having been worked on by man. . . . Even the way they [i.e., humans] see and hear is inseparable from the social life-process as it has evolved over the millennia. The facts which our senses present to us are socially preformed in two ways: through the historical character of the object perceived and through the historical character of the perceiving organ.

Thus, what we see (the objects of science) and how we see (science) are shaped by their social and historical context. Horkheimer (ibid., 222) continues: 'The critical theory of society . . . has for its object men [sic] as producers of their own historical way of life in its totality'. The object of critical theory is a historically created object, one that changes according to time and place, and therefore it should not be taken as second nature.

Critical Theory is not value neutral and does not pursue the ideal of value neutrality that is part and parcel of traditional theory. Horkheimer's critical theory does not accept the fact/value distinction or the distinction between descriptive and normative. Instead it is interested. The scientist – including the critical theorist – has interests, and science itself has political consequences. One must therefore clarify these interests and choose to work for the right interests: 'the critical theory . . . very consciously makes its own that concern for the rational organization of human activity' (ibid., 223).[2] And Horkheimer (ibid., 224) continues: 'the [critical] theory never aims simply at an increase of knowledge as such. Its goal is man's emancipation from slavery'. Critical theory must be both diagnostic and remedial. It has a practical interest in social change, and this is possible because it does not take society as second nature. There is a dialectic between how the world is and how we view the world. So, a final defining characteristic of critical theory is self-reflexivity. Theory must reflect on the fact that it is itself a social practice and that it always comes hand in hand with certain interests. The flipside of this is that for critical theory, the subject/object distinction is blurred. You do not have a subject (the scientist) isolated from the object (society). Rather, social science (and indeed all science) itself becomes part of its object of study.

With this, Critical Theory can be summed up in six points: (1) it analyses contemporary society, which it characterizes as capitalist, even if not exclusively so; (2) it takes the ambiguous nature of progress as a central point of inquiry; (3) it takes society as a totality and examines all areas of society; (4) it is interdisciplinary; (5) it combines philosophy and empirical social science; and (6) it is self-reflexive.

At the end of this chapter, I shall ask whether Habermas is a critical theorist in the sense of critical theory presented here. Now, however, I will turn to Habermas's critique of Horkheimer and Adorno.

HABERMAS'S CRITIQUE OF HORKHEIMER AND ADORNO

Although Habermas always had his disagreements with Horkheimer and Adorno, he did not publish any lengthy, direct critique of them until the 1980s by which time they were dead and Habermas had developed his own approach to critical theory (Habermas 1984, 345–55, 366–99; 1987c, chapter 5; 1993, chapter 4).

Habermas shares many concerns with Horkheimer and Adorno, above all the Critical Theory approach to philosophy and social science outlined above. Habermas's (1987c, 118f) main criticism of Horkheimer and Adorno is that their critique of modernity and reason take on a totalizing form. This renders it impotent, in particular because it does not leave them with an alternative. The problem is this: Horkheimer and Adorno identify reason as a defining part of modernity, and they identify reason with instrumental (or purposive) reason. Instrumental reason reduces our relationship to the world to one of a subject trying to dominate an object. The same happens when reason is applied in the context of humans and social relations. When (instrumental) reason is applied in this area, humans are treated as objects to be manipulated and dominated. Thus, modernity equals reason, reason equals instrumental reason, and instrumental reason equals manipulation and domination.

For Habermas (ibid.), this account of modernity and reason raises two questions. The first question is: where is the alternative? Horkheimer and Adorno seem caught within an 'iron cage' of reason *qua* domination, to paraphrase Weber. They have nowhere to turn for emancipation from the alienation and domination they associate with modernity and reason. Here they differ from Marx, who, after all, located an emancipatory force at the heart of capitalist exploitation: when the proletariat has nothing to loose but its chains, it will create a new social order. Marx's solution to the problem with capitalism is inherent to capitalism itself: capitalism creates its own grave-diggers, as he says. Likewise Habermas believes that, whatever the problems with modernity and reason, it is within these that we shall also find a way out of those problems. Thus he proposes a differentiated notion of reason, where instrumental reason is but one kind of reason, and so he rests his hopes on another kind of reason – namely, communicative reason – as an emancipatory force. For Habermas, Horkheimer's total rejection of reason leads to defeatism.

The second question Habermas raises against Horkheimer and Adorno's critique of modernity and reason is this: if Horkheimer and Adorno dismiss reason, what are they themselves engaged in? Presumably they are engaged in some kind of reasoning, in a Critical Theory style. But then they get caught in what Habermas calls a 'performative contradiction'. What they say (reason is domination) contradicts the assumptions on which their actions rely (they must assume that they can convince others by reasoning rather than through domination).

The performative contradiction argument is an argument Habermas brings to bear on those who, he says, argue against the force of arguments. The performative contradiction takes the following form: 'A performative contradiction occurs when a constative speech act $k(p)$ rests on noncontingent presuppositions whose propositional content contradicts the asserted proposition p' (Habermas 1990, 80). Habermas's point is that, in their critique and description of reason as domination, Horkheimer and Adorno rely on assumptions about the possibility of critique that they simultaneously reject. He writes about their dismissal of reason that 'this description of the self-destruction of the critical capacity [of reason] is paradoxical, because in the moment of description [of reason as domination] it still has to make use of the critique that has been declared dead'. The result is that critique becomes impotent when it is 'totalized' (Habermas 1987c, 119).

Habermas must stake out an alternative foundation for critique. Yet, at the same time, and like Horkheimer and Adorno, he rejects the essentialism and teleology of, for instance, Marx. In this sense, Habermas is a post-foundationalist theorist. What that 'foundation' can be I will return to in the last section of this chapter.

We can sum up Habermas's critique of Horkheimer and Adorno by adding that Habermas's diagnosis of contemporary society is nowhere as bleak as theirs. Habermas can be scathing in his critique of contemporary society, especially in his earlier work. This is the case in *The Structural Transformation of the Public Sphere* (1989a, parts VI–VII) when he criticizes the post-World War II public sphere and the way in which it is 'managed' by the big media corporations. However, he sees a light in the darkness. That light is not Marx's proletariat because Habermas rejects important parts of the Marxist analysis of capitalism and history. Instead, Habermas sees the light in what Horkheimer and Adorno believes is the problem: reason.

However, when Habermas talks about reason, it is not reason as Horkheimer and Adorno understand it. In Chapters 3 and 4, I shall say more about how Habermas developed his alternative conception of reason during the 1970s, in *The Theory of Communicative Action* (1984; 1987a) and 'Discourse Ethics' (in 1990), but some brief remarks are in place at this point.

Most importantly, Habermas has a differentiated and procedural notion of reason. At a basic level, Habermas differentiates between instrumental and communicative reason. Instrumental reason is modelled on a subject–object relation, and the aim is manipulation and domination of the object, whether the latter is nature or other human beings. Communicative reason is intersubjective. It aims at shared understanding and consensus on the basis of domination-free dialogue. That is, communicative reason is a matter of subject–subject relationships where one treats the other not merely as a means to an end, but as an end in itself, to paraphrase Kant. In communicative reason, there is thus an inbuilt ideal of freedom and equality, and this can form the basis of critique.

So, for Habermas, the possibility of critique, and of saving reason from Horkheimer and Adorno's totalizing critique of it, rests on the ability to distinguish different kinds of reason, and of distinguishing domination from the ideal of a consensus based on a domination free dialogue. Habermas believes that the latter is inherent to social relations, even if it is rarely realized in practice, and it is on this that he bases his optimism. If we work with a differentiated notion of reason, and if we focus on rationalization in the context of communicative reason, then there is hope.

Habermas not only differentiates the notion of reason, but also argues for a procedural notion of reason. What is rational is not this or that proposition, but any proposition that can stand the test of procedures conceived as discourses in which arguments are tried and rejected or accepted. Rationality becomes a characteristic of the procedures for achieving truth and normative rightness rather than the characteristic of a specific outcome. I return to the full argument for procedural rationality in Chapters 3 and 4.

Here we also get a good idea of how Habermas works. Although Habermas is critical of contemporary society, he finds in its institutions and practices a set of immanent ideals that can be held up against those institutions and practices. For instance, communicative reason may not be realized in practice, but it is something that we must, according to Habermas, at least presume. Thus it is 'real' and can be used as a critical yardstick to measure and criticize structures, institutions and practices. In this, Habermas (for instance, 1987c, 117) has learned from the early Marx's use of bourgeois ideals as a critical lever against bourgeois society.

In his critique of Horkheimer and Adorno, Habermas uses the performative contradiction argument, which is not unrelated to the Marxian critique of bourgeois society. He uses it to show that they must presume what they otherwise deny, namely that reason cannot be reduced to domination. More generally, Habermas builds his own theoretical framework through an engagement with other theorists, whether philosophers or social, political or legal theorists. His engagement is therefore not historical, but reconstructive. He points out contradictions in their thinking and reconstructs their arguments according to his own problematic (for instance, can reason be salvaged from its own negative tendencies?). Thus, his interest in other theorists is to learn from them, to see what they can contribute to his own version of a critical theory of society.

KNOWLEDGE AND HUMAN INTERESTS

The first step in Habermas's development of a critical theory of society was taken with the idea of 'human interests' or 'knowledge constitutive interests'. This idea is most developed in *Knowledge and*

Human Interests (1987b), first published in 1968. Later Habermas rejected most of the programme of *Knowledge and Human Interests*, but it is useful to briefly examine it because it formed part of Habermas's debate with positivism and hermeneutics, and the later communicative turn was partly in response to problems with this earlier programme.

To get an idea of what Habermas wants to achieve with the idea of 'knowledge constitutive interests', one can begin with his critique of positivism (Habermas 1987b, chapters 4–6; see also Habermas 1984; 1988a). Positivism has long been the dominant paradigm in the natural sciences, and it also has a dominant standing among many social scientists. Habermas is critical of the claims that positivist philosophy of science makes for positivism. He also refers to it as 'scientism'. I shall focus here on two points that Habermas levels at positivism.

First of all, the fact/value distinction. Positivism seeks to rescue the scientific and neutral status of its knowledge by distinguishing fact from value. Science should and can be value neutral – in short, disinterested. The scientist should, for instance, abstract from his or her values and ideology, from what Habermas (1988a, 265) sarcastically calls 'the sewage of emotionality'. Since positivism presupposes that it is itself value neutral, it is blind to the possibility that it may in fact rest on a set of particular values or even be infested with ideology. This is precisely what Habermas (ibid., 269) argues is the case. Positivism is secretly committed to the values of efficiency and economy. These are in turn the values of a particular order, namely the capitalist one, because as long as we pursue only these values it serves to reproduce the capitalist order. So, positivism is in fact ideological and interested, but it is unable to reflect on its own social interest, and this is, as we saw, one of the mainstays of critical theory: its self-reflexivity and acknowledgement that science is part of society and, as such, part of what science studies.

Habermas's second main criticism of positivism is that it takes one specific category of knowledge (and reason), namely empirical–analytical knowledge, as a model of all knowledge. Empirical–analytical knowledge is based on the human capacity to labour, but human life is more than labour and the instrumental rationality that goes hand in hand with it.

Here we arrive at the notion of interests. Habermas believes that it is necessary to work with a notion of interests. For instance, one can use a notion of interests to show how positivism is interested, and that it has a particular interest in certain values and in a certain social order. However, Habermas rejects the Marxist notion of interests as tied to class. The class structure of contemporary societies is more complex than Marx allowed for, and class is tied to labour which is just one aspect of life. Thereby the Marxist analysis of interests becomes too narrow (Habermas 1987b, chapter 3). Indeed, Habermas argues that science is not simply bourgeois because it can be put to use for other interests. Yet, science is not neutral either. It is tied to one aspect of human life and activity, namely labour, or what we do with nature, so it is tied to a subject–object relationship.

Habermas asks himself what would happen if we expand and differentiate the notion of interests to other aspects of human life. He is interested in the transcendental conditions of possibility of knowledge, that is, in what makes knowledge possible. Importantly, unlike Kant but like Hegel and Marx, Habermas believes that this question cannot be dissociated from an analysis of society (hence he talks about '*quasi*-transcendental' conditions of knowledge). What constitutes knowledge is not fixed, but historical, and Habermas (ibid., 195–7, 312) links it to a history of the development of the species. This is what Habermas (ibid., 196) has in mind when he writes:

> I term *interests* the basic orientations rooted in specific fundamental conditions of the possible reproduction and self-constitution of the human species . . . Knowledge-constitutive interests can be defined exclusively as a function of the objectively constituted problems of the preservation of life that have been solved by the cultural form of existence as such.

In short, through the ways in which we reproduce human life, we develop certain basic, human interests, which can vary historically because society has developed.

In another place, Habermas (ibid., 311) writes: 'Because science must secure the objectivity of its statements against the pressure and seduction of particular interests, it deludes itself about the fundamental interests to which it owes not only its impetus but *the conditions of possible objectivity themselves.*' In other words, science must reflect on the knowledge constitutive interests that make scientific knowledge possible in the first place. This is the idea of human or knowledge constitutive interests. Importantly, for Habermas there is not one human interest, but interest*s* in the plural. Habermas (ibid., 308–13) makes a tripartite distinction between three interests, which in turn correspond to three kinds of knowledge and three kinds of human activity.

There is, first, an interest in technical control over objective nature, which is linked to instrumental reason and purposive-rational action. It is linked to the human activity of labour, and one finds this kind of knowledge pursued in the natural sciences modelled on positivism. For Habermas, there is nothing wrong with this interest as such, but one should neither reduce human interests to this particular interest in technical control nor reduce human activity to labour. Consequently, for Habermas one should not reduce science and knowledge to natural science or positivism. By differentiating the notions of interests, reason and knowledge, Habermas hopes to be able to salvage the potential for progress that is after all associated with technical control.

Second, there is an interest in mutual understanding, and this is linked by Habermas to communicative reason and communicative action. It is linked to interaction in the lifeworld, and this kind of knowledge is pursued by the hermeneutical sciences. From hermeneutics, Habermas takes the idea that one must go through the language and the self-descriptions of the agents that one is studying. However, for Habermas (1980; 1983; 1984, 53–66), the problem with the hermeneutics of someone like Hans-Georg Gadamer and Peter Winch is that it takes consensus as given. By starting from a given tradition, hermeneutics is unable to judge whether that tradition, consensus or language is systematically distorted. In short, even though we have to go through the self-descriptions of the agents we are studying, we cannot simply trust those self-descriptions. We need to be able to reach beyond those self-descriptions because the agents may be delusional about themselves and the world. Their self-descriptions may be ideological in a way they cannot themselves see through. The question is how Habermas can provide a critical point of view that does not step outside of language. His answer is that any attempt at hermeneutical interpretation presupposes an appeal to universal pragmatic standards of language, which I shall come back to shortly.

The third human interest is an interest in emancipation from domination and in autonomy in the sense of being in control of the conditions under which one lives. Habermas uses Marx and Freud as examples of investigations that have pursued this interest in emancipation (for Habermas on Freud, see Habermas 1987b, chapters 10–12). In both cases, they try to unmask structures that are otherwise hidden from the view of the agents. In this sense, they provide a solution to the problems associated with hermeneutics. They seek to raise agents' self-consciousness of underlying structures in order to dispel distortion and alienation. Where the other two human interests are linked to labour and language respectively, the interest in emancipation is linked to power.

THE TURN TO COMMUNICATION

From the early 1970s onwards, Habermas puts the programme of human, or knowledge constitutive, interests behind him as a response to criticisms of that programme. Recall that Habermas referred to the quasi-transcendental human interests as the presuppositions of possible objective knowledge. He did so from the perspective of the history of the reproduction of the human species, a history that can be understood as a learning process – hence why he refers to *human* interests. The cognitive human interests are at once empirical and transcendental, thus continuing the Critical Theory tradition of locating regulative and critical ideals in existing practices. Through self-reflection and awareness of the universal interests, you acquire freedom from 'the pressure and seduction of particular interests' (ibid., 311).

However, the programme of human interests remained within what Habermas calls the philosophy of the subject, or the philosophy of consciousness, and the related problems of self-reflection. This is a critique Habermas develops with his turn to communication. The general point is this: if you start from a subject (or a consciousness), then rationality becomes a matter of either decisionism (it comes down to what the subject decides) or a means–end rationality where the natural and social world become objects for the subject. The problem is, according to Habermas, that what is rational for a subject can ultimately only be grasped from the perspective of that subject. Instead, he argues, we must shift to an intersubjective perspective, one that starts from the relations among subjects, and that means turning to language and communication.

Since the starting point of the earlier programme of human interests was a philosophy of the subject, the emancipation of the subject was supposed to result from a process of *self*-reflection. The subject in question was the human species, and this subject was supposed to pull itself out of ignorance and alienation. However, this raises the question of how a subject (here, the human species) that is not yet emancipated can achieve the goal of emancipating itself. Either the subject does not already have an interest in its own emancipation, but then it will be unable to carry out the process of self-reflection on its own (here the solution may be philosophical paternalism and/or political avant-gardism). Or the subject does have an interest in its own emancipation, but then the risk is that this interest teleologically foreshadows the process of the subject's self-reflection and subsequent emancipation (the self-reflection will take place behind the back of the subject, who is supposed to carry it out).[3] The actual self-reflection can only be carried out by the subjects themselves, and so the problem is to show how the subjects can transcend their own ignorance and alienation, without the philosopher (Habermas, for example) handing down their emancipation to them in a paternalistic manner.

Habermas's turn to a formal pragmatics of language and, subsequently, a discourse theory of ethics and democracy was meant to solve these problems. Habermas announces the paradigm shift from a philosophy of the subject to an intersubjective philosophy, from a philosophy of consciousness to a philosophy of language in the following manner: 'Today the problem of language has replaced the traditional problem of consciousness; the transcendental critique of language supersedes that of consciousness.' (Habermas 1988c, 117) The beginnings of this alternative are already present in Habermas's inaugural lecture at Frankfurt in 1965. There he says:

> The human interest in autonomy and responsibility is not mere fancy, for it can be apprehended a priori. What raises us out of nature is the only thing whose nature we can know: *language*. Through its structure, autonomy and responsibility are posited for us. Our first sentence expresses unequivocally the intention of universal and unconstrained consensus. (Habermas 1987b, 314)

In *Knowledge and Human Interests*, Habermas makes the tripartite distinction between labour, language and power. Here, and subsequently, he links emancipation and autonomy to language, and to the implicit but inherent aim of language, namely consensus on the basis of a domination free discourse. Habermas thus stakes his bets on language as the basis for critical theory, and this has subsequently let others, both critical theorists and theorists working within different traditions, to criticize Habermas for ignoring the areas of labour and power.[4]

After *Knowledge and Human Interests*, Habermas moves from transcendental analysis (of knowledge constitutive interests as the conditions of knowledge) to the analysis of the pragmatic structure of language. This is in response to another problem with the earlier programme. In *Knowledge and Human Interests*, Habermas was concerned with how objects are and must be constituted in order for certain kinds of knowledge to be possible. He was not concerned with validity (truth) apart from truth understood as self-reflection. So, subjects will be emancipated through self-reflection because they and their social context will become transparent, for instance, when they no longer take bourgeois rights to be natural or the only ones possible.

Subsequently, Habermas (ibid., 377f.) distinguishes between reflection and reconstruction. He uses the reconstructive method in both his discourse ethics and his theory of deliberative democracy. Rational reconstructions aim to reconstruct the underlying and implicit structures of social interaction (Habermas 1990, 1–42; 1998, 21–46). In his theory of discourse ethics, Habermas uses a 'formal pragmatic analysis, which focuses on the general and necessary conditions for the validity of symbolic expressions and achievements'. He looks at how rationality and validity can be discursively generated (Habermas 1990, 31).[5] In the theory of deliberative democracy, he seeks to rationally reconstruct the implicit principles of constitutional democracy (see Chapter 5). The reconstructed structures, or presuppositions, are constitutive in the sense that there are no alternatives to them: we cannot but take them for granted.

In rational reconstructions, philosophy and '[e]mpirical theories with strong universalistic claims' converge (Habermas 1990, 15; see also 1987a, 399f). Philosophy and reconstructive empirical sciences work in tandem, one checking the always fallible results of the other – again a recurring theme among Frankfurt School critical theorists. Reconstructive philosophy and social science should avoid, on the one hand, an empiricism that offers no critical distance from the present and, on the other hand, a transcendentalism that simply superimposes its categories onto reality. This is why Habermas talks about the *quasi*-transcendental status of the reconstructed universals.

Reconstruction is only one side of this general shift. The other side is reflection, which takes the form of discursive testing of validity claims. According to Habermas's theory of discourse ethics, it is up to the agents themselves to test validity claims to truth and normative rightness in discourses. Rationality is a characteristic of the discourses, and truth and normative rightness cannot be imposed by a philosopher who claims to know better. Similarly, in deliberative democracy, citizens give themselves their own laws. Here we see the central theme of Habermas's work, namely the public use of reason understood as the force of the better argument.

However, this begs the question of the rationality of the discourses, and this is precisely what rational reconstructions of universal and unavoidable structures of communication are supposed to solve. The rational reconstructions set out the conditions under which subjects and citizens may rationally decide the validity of claims to truth and normative rightness. The critical self-reflection of the programme of human interests thus divides into two, namely rational reconstruction and the discursive testing of validity claims.

Whether Habermas pulls this argument off is a matter of contention. Here I shall just highlight one potential problem, namely the potential clash between the perspectives of, on one side, the philosopher and the social scientist and, on the other side, the social agents. The danger is that the philosopher and the social scientist impose what they claim to be universal structures on social agents in a paternalistic way. There was a similar problem with human interests and self-reflection, and it does not go away with the division of labour between philosopher/social scientist and social agents.

Habermas's (1990, 32) answer to this problem is to say that rational reconstructions are fallible and hypothetical, just like the validity claims or the consensus that participants in discourse arrive at: '*all* rational reconstructions, like other types of knowledge, have only hypothetical status. There is always the possibility that they rest on a false choice of examples, that they are obscuring and distorting correct intuitions, or, more frequently, that they are overgeneralizing individual cases'. These are practical problems that can, in principle, be overcome, and the philosopher/social scientist must herself submit her findings to discursive testing among her peers in the scientific community.

Later, in Chapters 3 and 4, I shall give a fuller account of how Habermas unfolds the communicative turn and of how he reworks critical theory in this mould. All that remains to note is that through this change to a communicative, intersubjectivist paradigm, Habermas hopes to resuscitate a strong link between empirical and transcendental inquiry, and to base a Critical Theory on this. This is how Habermas (1987b, 380) himself puts it at the end of a postscript discussing the limitations of the earlier programme in *Knowledge and Human Interests*:

> [T]he cleavage between a real and an inevitable idealized (if only hypothetically ideal) community of language is built not only into the process of argumentative reasoning but into the very life-praxis of social systems. In this way, perhaps the Kantian notion of the fact of reason can be revitalized.

The commitment to defending one's validity claims to one's peers in domination free discourse and to reach a consensus is not something one chooses, but an inherent *telos* of language itself, and language is in turn an inherent part of what it means to be human.

FURTHER READINGS

The two books by Habermas that are most relevant for the topics of this chapter – *Theory and Practice* (1988) and *Knowledge and Human Interests* (1987b) – are heavily loaded with philosophical jargon, and both are difficult reads. Thomas McCarthy's (1978) introduction to Habermas's earlier work, *The Critical Theory of Jürgen Habermas*, is an excellent, if advanced introduction. The same goes for Garbis Kortian's *Metacritique* (1980) and Raymond Geuss's (1981) *The Idea of Critical Theory*. For critical discussions of Habermas and critical theory, see *Habermas: Critical Debates,* edited by John B. Thompson and David Held (1982), *Habermas and Modernity*, edited by Richard Bernstein (1985) and *Jürgen Habermas. Volume I*, edited by David Rasmussen and James Swindal (2002a).

CHAPTER TWO

THE PUBLIC SPHERE

INTRODUCTION

The Structural Transformation of the Public Sphere is one of the best-known books by Habermas (1989a), and Habermas is often thought of as the theorist of the public sphere. It was Habermas's *Habilitationsschrift* at the Faculty of Philosophy at the University of Marburg in what was then West Germany. Originally, Habermas was meant to do his *Habilitationsschrift* in Frankfurt at the Institute for Social Research. However, Horkheimer, the then leader of the Institute, was critical of Habermas's approach. He thought Habermas was not critical enough of the culture industry that Horkheimer had criticized so devastatingly with Adorno in *Dialectic of Enlightenment* (Horkheimer and Adorno 2002). He also thought that Habermas's solutions for overcoming the problems in the contemporary public sphere were a tat too radical. Consequently, Habermas went to Marburg where he did his *Habilitationsschrift* with the openly radical and Marxist scholar Wolfgang Abendroth.

The Structural Transformation of the Public Sphere was published in German in 1962, but translated into English only in 1989. The late English translation of the book is odd because it had long been translated into several other languages. What is more, the book had an immense impact in Germany and initiated a range of discussions in academia and in the media.[1] With its critique of contemporary Western late capitalist societies, the book struck a chord with a new generation of students and academics. It is also a relatively easily accessible book because of its historical and sociological detail. As such, it appealed to a wider, non-academic audience than Habermas's later and more theoretical works. The discussions of the book were not restricted to the German speaking world though. Through Habermas's Anglo-Saxon (and mainly American) interlocutors, the arguments of the book travelled – by way of a critical reception – into the English speaking world as well.

The book is a good example of critical theory in practice. It examines the emergence of the bourgeois public sphere, its ideological structure, and its eventual demise as a sphere for rational debate. It is an example of critical theory for several reasons. First of all, it is interdisciplinary, drawing on a range of disciplines: history, sociology, psychology, philosophy and political science. Habermas (1989a, xvii) himself says, in the 'Author's Preface', that were it not for this interdisciplinary approach, he would not have been able to capture the complexity of the public sphere in its historical and contemporary forms.

Linked to this, the book is both historical, examining the historical emergence, consolidation and demise of the public sphere, and sociological in that it locates an ideal of the public sphere which transcends its particular historical forms (ibid., xvii–xviii). What is more, the book proceeds as an immanent critique of the bourgeois public sphere. That is, Habermas criticizes the biases and exclusions of the public sphere as it has emerged and especially in its contemporary form. He does so on the basis of an ideal of the public sphere – as the site of rational communication – which he locates in the very historical practices he is also criticizing. Thus, the public sphere is held up against its own, immanent ideal. This is the idea of immanent critique that one finds in many critical theorists going back to Karl Marx.

Habermas's point concerning the bourgeois public sphere is that, although the public sphere is marked by biases and exclusions, and although the idea of the public sphere as a sphere of equality and inclusion is an ideological cover for the bourgeoisie's economic interests, the public sphere is more than ideology. It is also an ideal that can be used to criticize the ideological aspects of the public sphere as well as its biases and exclusions. Notice also how Habermas, in another move characteristic of Critical Theory, locates the potential for reason and emancipation in a particular practice and institution within society. That is, he finds a beam of hope in an otherwise criticizable society, a beam of hope that is capable of transcending contemporary society and its injustice because it can show us a way out of them.

In this chapter, I shall first present Habermas's historical and sociological account of the emergence, consolidation and decline of the bourgeois public sphere in *The Structural Transformation of the Public Sphere*. I then consider two clusters of criticisms and Habermas's responses to them. I first present criticisms that Habermas is too optimistic and idealizing in his description of the initial public sphere in the seventeenth, eighteenth and nineteenth centuries, and that he overlooks the significance of the exclusions of, for instance, women for the structure of the public sphere. Second, I present the criticism that Habermas is too pessimistic about the contemporary state of the public sphere. Habermas reacts to this by developing a more positive account of the role of the public sphere in his theory of deliberative democracy. Finally, in the last two sections, I present an example that sheds light on Habermas's theory of the public sphere, while also highlighting some of the limits to it, namely his involvement in debates about student politics in the 1960s.

THE EMERGENCE OF THE BOURGEOIS PUBLIC SPHERE

The Structural Transformation of the Public Sphere is about just that: how the bourgeois public sphere has transformed – that is, changed – over the last centuries. Strictly speaking 'the structural transformation of the public sphere' refers to the decay and disintegration of the public sphere during the last hundred or so years. It can also be taken to refer more generally to the way the public sphere has changed, though: how it emerged in the seventeenth and eighteenth centuries, how it was consolidated in the eighteenth century and first half of the nineteenth century, and how it then started disintegrating with the inclusion of the masses and the expansion of the state from the late nineteenth century onwards. The book follows this structure of the 'rise and fall' of the public sphere. Habermas first explains how it emerged with capitalist society, its structure and ideas that constituted it in its prime, and then its gradual decay and disintegration. I shall follow the same structure in the explanation of the central theses of the book in the following.

The bourgeois public sphere emerged hand in hand with the gradual advent of capitalism from the seventeenth century onwards, although at different paces in different countries. Before examining how it emerges, it is useful to contrast it with, first, the situation in the advanced ancient Greek city states and, second, the situation in feudal Europe. This will give a clearer picture of this *modern, bourgeois* public sphere.

The bourgeois public sphere relies on a distinction between private and public. The public sphere is precisely public, as distinguished from the private world of either the family (what Habermas refers to as the sphere of intimacy) or the market, where agents compete for profit. The Greek city state also relied on a division between the private and the public. There the private belonged to the home, the *oikos*, which was characterized by necessity (food, reproduction and so on). The *oikos* was the sphere of women and slaves, who were not citizens, and the head of the *oikos* was male and a citizen. As citizens, they would come together in the public sphere to deliberate and to govern, often by turn.

The bourgeois public sphere opposes itself not just to the private sphere but also to the state (which, today, is also sometimes referred to as public as in 'public servant', 'public policy' and the 'public sector'). At first, the bourgeois public sphere worked as a check on government, taking care of society's general interests against the particular interests of the ruler(s). Later the public sphere became the basis for government as the idea was that the laws should be based on rational will, which would in turn emerge from the rational debate of the public sphere. Thus, one difference between the public sphere of the ancient Greek city states and the bourgeois public sphere is that the latter is opposed to the state, but is not limited from debating economic issues (ibid., 3f.).

The bourgeois public sphere is also distinguished from its feudal predecessor. There 'public' referred to the ruler or aristocracy who would represent themselves before – often literally in front of – the people, their subjects. The public sphere was the place where the rulers were recognized as the rightful rulers, and the people did not have an active role in this. It was a staged and managed public sphere. Later, Habermas will talk about the re-feudalization of the public sphere in the twentieth century. By this he means that the citizens (now 'the public') become passive consumers of infotainment and that their only role is to acclaim the ruling elites' decisions. This is opposed to the bourgeois public sphere where the public use of reasons by the citizens themselves becomes the source of legitimacy within society (ibid., 5–14). The bourgeois public sphere supposedly consists of an active citizenry, who consider themselves to be the source of legitimate government.

The bourgeois public sphere emerges with capitalism, and like capitalism it emerges gradually. With capitalism a new class appears alongside the aristocracy and the peasants. This new class of capitalists – the bourgeoisie – is primarily based in the towns and cities. At first, they are engaged in trade, and later they start what is more properly speaking capitalist production. In this sense, the bourgeois public sphere has a definite social and economic basis. However, Habermas wants to avoid the orthodoxy of the Marxist base-superstructure model. He argues that the bourgeois public sphere cannot be reduced to its class basis because it contains a claim to universal inclusion. However formal and fictional that claim may be, it still means that otherwise excluded groups can use this ideal as a wager against whatever de facto exclusions may exist. I return to this at more length below.

The early stages of capitalism saw the appearance of traders, but they traded within structures that were in many respects still feudal. Only gradually did they become more independent and also start to trade between towns and beyond. This in turn gave rise to a need for regulation that was uniform and predictable across different towns and at a national level. To be efficient, the new trade capitalism needed some uniformity in the laws and in tax matters so that they could act under conditions that were predictable. Here we find one of the reasons for the emergence of the state at a national level. At first, the state promoted trade, later it promoted production as well. In both cases, the state is at once distinguished from, and supportive of, the market.

The non-state sphere was divided too. Production gradually ceased to take place within the confines of the household and the family. People became agents in the market as buyers and sellers of commodities and labour, and production was moved physically to factories. One result was that production was no longer solely a private concern (of the family or of the individual capitalist), but also a public concern which the state had to promote. Another result was a division between the economic sphere and the sphere of intimacy, most notably the family.

The public sphere that emerged did so hand in hand with these developments. With trade and production came a desire and need for predictability and also for information – in short, for news. Traders and producers needed information about infrastructure, prices, taxes and so on. The trade itself provided one communication channel for this information, but gradually newsletters emerged. These were also used by the state and the courts to spread information. They carried information about markets and so on, but they also carried other news that was not strictly economic (ibid., 14–26).

Next, a literary public sphere emerged. This was closely linked to the bourgeois family, both as a consumer of literature and as a source of the relationships depicted in the literature. Literature was a mirror in which the bourgeois class reflected on its norms and its place in society. The literature – which appeared in books, journals and periodicals – was aimed at a general public, however, and it was produced cheaply, which was made possible by new printing techniques. Unlike earlier literature and feudal society, the new literature gained its authority from its readers, or rather from its readers' critical appropriation of it. Thus, the new literature was not considered good (or bad) as a matter of nature or by religious or royal decree. Rather, the literature and its value came to be something to be debated. What was debated was value and everybody in the literary public sphere was supposed to have taste and therefore supposed to be able to make value judgments about what they read. So, what emerged was an idea of critique, and this critique could be rational.

This is important because it ushered in a critical public, a public trained in critical discussions, even if initially only in the field of literature. Eventually this critical public started debating matters beyond the sphere of intimacy, just as they started debating things beyond what had to do with their private businesses in a narrow sense. In this way, politics, law and government also became matters of taste and value – in short, matters about which citizens could arrive at rational solutions on the basis of critical debate (ibid., chapters 6–7).

Also key to Habermas's account here are the coffeehouses (in Britain), salons (in France) and table societies (in Germany). In these institutions, members of the bourgeoisie – almost exclusively men – met to discuss issues of the day, whether they were gossip, information about prices, novels – or politics. Together with the press in its different forms (newsletters, periodicals, books and so on), these meeting places formed the institutional basis for the bourgeois public sphere.[2]

Habermas's account of the emergence of the bourgeois public sphere is very rich, and it is impossible to do justice to the detailed character of his account here. What should be clear are the basics: the bourgeois public sphere emerged with capitalism and the new class of capitalist traders and producers; it was distinguished from the sphere of the market, from the sphere of intimacy and from the state, although it also interacted with, and drew upon, these in important ways; and its institutional basis was in the press and the coffeehouses. In the following section, I turn to look at how Habermas characterizes the public sphere and the tensions that define it. Before that, a few comments are necessary on its historical emergence, though.

It would be easy to see the public sphere as a class phenomenon – as the *bourgeois* public sphere, emerging on the back of the bourgeois class and capitalist trade and production. There is something to be said for such an interpretation, and later we shall see how this class basis gives rise to exclusions. However, Habermas stresses that the public sphere is not so much the public sphere of a particular class of people as the public sphere of bourgeois *society*. This does not take away from its bias and exclusivity, but it does mean that the ideas behind the public sphere leave it – at least formally – open to other groups in society. Thus, initially, aristocrats were frequent participants in the literary and political discussions in the press and in the coffeehouses. What remains is a sphere that is taken by its members to be distinctive from the sphere of intimacy, from the sphere of production and need, and from the state. It is a sphere that is taken to be opposed to and a check on the state. Habermas (ibid., 24) writes:

> Because, on the one hand, the society now confronting the state clearly separated a private domain from public authority and because, on the other hand, it turned the reproduction of life into something transcending the confines of private domestic authority and becoming a subject of public interest, that zone of continuous administrative contact became 'critical' also in the sense that it provoked the critical judgment of a public making use of its own reason.

Progressively, the public sphere was seen as not only a check on government, but as the rational basis for government. '[T]he critical judgement of a public making use of its own reason' became the source of legitimacy in society. This takes us to the idea and ideology underlying the consolidated form of the public sphere.

THE IDEA AND IDEOLOGY OF THE PUBLIC SPHERE

Habermas (ibid., 27) initially characterizes the bourgeois public sphere as follows:

> The bourgeois public sphere may be conceived above all as the sphere of private people come together as a public; they soon claimed the public sphere regulated from above against the public authorities themselves, to engage them in a debate over the general rules governing relations in the basically privatized but publicly relevant sphere of commodity exchange and social labour. The medium of this political confrontation was peculiar and without historical precedent: people's use of their reason (*öffentliches Räsonnement*).

The self-understanding on the part of the public sphere expressed in this and the previous quote is also famously expressed by Immanuel Kant in 'An Answer to the Question: "What is Enlightenment?"'. There Kant (1991a, 54) writes:

> *Enlightenment is man's emergence from his self-incurred immaturity. Immaturity* is the inability to use one's own understanding without the guidance of another. This immaturity is *self-incurred* if its cause is not lack of understanding, but lack of resolution and courage to use it without the guidance of another. The motto of enlightenment is therefore: *Sapere aude!* Have courage to use your *own* understanding!

In other words, the self-understanding of the public sphere could be expressed as: 'have courage to use your own critical reason in the public sphere!' and 'have courage to use the reasoning in the public sphere against the authorities!'

I have already noted how, according to Habermas, the agents of the public sphere see their activities as a check on government and even as the basis for good government. How can they believe so? And how can they believe in the force of the use of reason in the public sphere? There are three ideas central to the public sphere, and these three ideas provide the answer to these questions (Habermas 1989a, 36f.).

First of all, although the public sphere does not assume the equality of the agents (in social and economic status), it disregards inequalities.

It involved 'a kind of social intercourse that, far from presupposing the equality of status, disregarded status altogether. The tendency replaced the celebration of rank with a tact befitting equals' (ibid., 36). This is important. The public sphere (and, by extension, liberalism) does not eradicate differences and inequalities, but abstracts from them. It claims to be a sphere where differences and inequalities are irrelevant and do no count. To paraphrase Habermas, only the better argument counts.

Second, while the agents may have different interests based on their status, these interests were to be disregarded. Instead, what unites them is a common, sort of 'disinterested' interest in reason. This is the interest that is also expressed by Kant's enlightenment thinking. The only judge should be the public, that is, rational argument, which should not be biased by particular interests. And reason can be applied to all areas of society, including areas that had so far been the preserve of the ruler, state or church. Anything that could be construed as of common concern was to be subject to the public use of reason.

Third, the public sphere was 'in principle inclusive' (ibid., 37). The public sphere is obviously biased and based on exclusions: of women, of the poor, of non-whites, of the illiterate and so on. However, Habermas (1992a, 425–7) claims that the exclusions were not constitutive, in the sense that without these exclusions the public sphere could not exist. 'However exclusive the public might be in any given instance,' he writes, 'it could never close itself off entirely and become consolidated as a clique' (ibid., 37). The public sphere rested on ideas of equality, inclusion, reason and so on, which may have been only formal and hypocritical, but nonetheless they opened the door – in principle, if not in reality – to ever broader groups. This is so because of the formality of the requirements for taking part in the public sphere: any human being who could reason could take part in the debates. Inclusion was not given by birth or by your status in society, at least not formally. Even the beggar had the right to take part in public debate. Here we see a clear difference between Habermas's approach and a more traditional Marxist one. The Marxist would stress the difference between formal and actual inclusion and the superficiality of the former; for him, the right to partake in the deliberations in the public sphere would be like the right to stay at the Ritz: empty, as long as the material conditions are not in place. Habermas, while not blind to the actual exclusions from the public sphere, believes that the formal equality and universal inclusion holds out a promise for the transformation of the public sphere in a progressive direction.

The ideas – or ideals – of the public sphere were never realized in practice. They may be described as fictions. There are first the fictions of universal inclusion into, and of equality within, the public sphere. Linked to this, there is also the fiction of the independence of the public sphere: from the state, from the economic sphere and its inequality and exploitation and from the sphere of intimacy, where the male is the head of the household. This fiction of the independence or autonomy of the public sphere is the reverse side of the idea that, in the public sphere, inequalities of status are disregarded.

Civil society is easily presumed to be independent from the state. That, after all, is part of the point of the market and the public sphere: that they are free from state interference. Later on liberalists will complain about welfare state provisions and regulations of the market on precisely this basis. But it should be clear that the state interfered with civil society from the very beginning, whether as an impartial arbiter in the form of the courts and policing, or as provider of infrastructure, or simply by virtue of securing the market from interference through constitutionally secured individual freedom rights for property owners.

The fictions described here are related to two naturalizations, first of the market and second of the bourgeois individual. The market is taken to be the natural order of things with its (apparent) neutrality and equality and, hence, fairness. Thus, interference is taken to be unnatural, as meddling in the natural course of things. This idea is transferred to the public sphere understood as a market of ideas, where the better argument ('commodity' or business) wins the day. Again, interference by the state is taken as unnatural.

'As a privatized individual, the bourgeois was two things in one: owner of goods and persons and one human being among others, that is, *bourgeois* and *homme*' (ibid., 55). The bourgeois (white, property owning male) person comes to see himself and to be seen by others as the natural subject of humanity. 'Bourgeois' imperceptively merges with 'human', which is to say 'man'. When the bourgeois looks himself in the mirror he sees a human, not a particular gendered, class subject with a particular skin colour. Everybody can in principle be included as a (reasoning) human being, but to be a human being one must be like a bourgeois man. In principle, the day labourer too can look himself in the mirror and recognize himself as a bourgeois/ human being.

The upshot of this is an inherent tension within the bourgeois public sphere. On the one hand, it is biased and exclusive. On the other hand, the public sphere contains a promise of equality and universal inclusion. In the light of the bias and exclusions, the promise of equality and inclusion looks hypocritical and ideological. In the light of the promise of equality and inclusion, the bias and exclusions can be criticized and potentially overcome. This is precisely the strategy of early (liberal) feminism, such as that of Mary Wollstonecraft. The liberal feminists argue for equality and inclusion of women on the basis of the promise in liberalism and in the bourgeois revolutions, the promise of equal rights for all humans. Thus, they try to redefine what it means to be a human, that is, to resist the reduction of 'human' to 'man' so that 'human' can also contain 'woman' (Wollstonecraft 2004).

Before turning to the decay and disintegration of the public sphere, I would like briefly to consider how Habermas (1989a, chapters 13–15) positions his reading of the self-understanding of the public sphere in relation to five important philosophers of the eighteenth and nineteenth centuries: Kant, Hegel, Marx, Mill and Tocqueville.

Immanuel Kant (1724–1804) is arguably the most important philosopher of the public sphere at his time. One example of that is his small piece on the question 'What is Enlightenment?' (Kant 1991a). He sees a great potential in the public use of reason to form the basis for rational and just rule. However, he does not entirely trust that flesh and blood human beings will be able to lift themselves out of their 'immaturity' or 'tutelage', as he expresses it. He has two solutions, both of which are unsatisfactory from the point of view of the self-understanding of the public sphere as Habermas reconstructs it. First, Kant posits a teleological or natural course that history will take behind our backs, so to speak. This absolves human beings of responsibility, but also of freedom. Second, Kant introduces an element of paternalism in that he limits the reasoning public to male citizens who are financially independent (whom Kant refer to as 'active' as opposed to 'passive' citizens). And the reasoning public is further helped along by the enlightened philosopher and ruler.

For G.W.F. Hegel (1770–1831), civil society – including the public sphere – is conflictual. Therefore it is necessary for the state to reconcile the differences within civil society, something the public sphere cannot do because it would merely reflect these conflicts. The result, however, is state domination. Hegel is no friend of the public sphere Habermas writes about. At most, the public sphere becomes an educational tool in the hands of the state.

Karl Marx (1818–83) accepts Hegel's description of civil society as conflictual, but he rejects the Hegelian solution. The state is the extension of the interests of the ruling class, the bourgeoisie, and as such the state cannot reconcile the conflicts of civil society. Thus, a revolutionary transformation of society as a whole is necessary, a revolution that would do away with all conflicts, but therefore also usher in the spectre of a society as a harmonious totality. This would be a society where debate in the public sphere would be reduced to a leisure activity.

For John Stuart Mill (1806–73) and Alexis de Tocqueville (1805–59), on the contrary, harmony is not natural, conflict is. They both celebrate the hustle and bustle of civil society and the public sphere. But they have an ambiguous view of public debate nonetheless. Public debate at once carries a potential for rationality and is the spectacle of mere subjective opinions. As the latter, public opinion carries the danger of becoming the tyranny of the majority. Hence, both Mill and Tocqueville argue for representative democracy to guard against the uneducated masses. Like Kant, Mill and Tocqueville thus reflect the tension in the self-understanding of the bourgeois public sphere, which is at once open to all and limited to educated and independent bourgeois.

THE DECLINE AND DISINTEGRATION OF THE PUBLIC SPHERE

The tension in the self-understanding of the bourgeois public sphere between *bourgeois* and *homme* eventually gives room for ever wider social groups gaining political rights and access to the public sphere. As a result, it was no longer possible to ignore the inequalities and injustices in society, and the state was now called upon to ameliorate these. This development, which Habermas dates back to the 1870s, gives rise to the modern welfare state. The result is that the division between state and civil society, which the bourgeoisie and the liberals had defended, breaks down. Private organizations assumed public power (the 'societalization of the state'), and the state penetrated the private realm (the 'state-ification of society') (Habermas 1992a, 432).

Increasingly, debate in the public sphere became debate over interests and over which and whose interests should prevail in public policy. Indeed, what used to be the site of rational-critical debate became the site of negotiation of interests, although this negotiation was increasingly hidden behind the closed doors of government, organizations and businesses. There was a shift from a universal, 'disinterested' interest in reason (however fictional) to the negotiation of particular interests.

This was part of the decline and disintegration – or what Habermas (1989a, 4) calls the 'decomposition' – of the public sphere. Other aspects of this decomposition concerned the role of consumption and political communication: 'rational-critical debate had a tendency to be replaced by consumption, and the web of public communication unravelled into acts of individuated reception, however uniform in mode' (ibid., 161). Where the public sphere was once made up of property owners and producers, it was now made up of agents who had a stable income of a certain level. They were first of all consumers. However, consumption is not mediated by rational-critical debate. All the consumer has to do is to 'justify' their consumption with reference to their subjective taste and to do so to themselves rather than to a public. Again we find an aspect of the decomposition or disintegration of the public sphere here. Consumption is individualized, both in the act of consuming and in the justification consumers give for their consumption. Similarly, although advertising is aimed at the masses, it is aimed at the masses as made up of individual, 'private' consumers who do not need to communicate with one another in order to consume.

Thus, where once the public sphere was organized around and oriented towards a common interest in reason and a common audience, interests and audience have now decomposed into a myriad of interests and audiences. The public sphere and rational-critical debate are substituted by advertising and so-called public relations. The public sphere not only become the generator for consumption, but its objects – opinions and information – themselves become objects of consumption by individuals who do not relate to them in a critical way.

Habermas refers to the 'refeudalization' of the public sphere. By this he means that the public sphere takes on characteristics it used to have in the feudal, pre-modern period. The public sphere becomes a representative public sphere in the sense that producers of information and opinions are divided from the consumers of information and opinions, and in the sense that the public sphere functions merely to acclaim the authority of particular opinions and pieces of information.

One example of this is the role of intellectuals. Earlier there was no sharp distinction between intellectuals – writers, critics and so on – and the wider public in the public sphere, because everybody addressed themselves to everybody. Later, a division emerged between those producing and those consuming literature, information, opinions and critique. The consumers of opinion are largely passive, and to the extent they are active, they are so as individuals and do not engage in critical dialogue with their peers or with the producers of opinions. The most extreme example of this would be the couch potato who watches (mostly poor entertainment, but also infotainment) television programmes from his private home and does not engage in critical debate about what he is watching (and in addition, he will be watching commercials for products – including further television programmes – which he will consume uncritically and individually).

The refeudalization thesis is more important when it comes to politics, though. There is, first, the emergence of the mass political parties, which are also bureaucratically and hierarchically organized, making it difficult to influence from the ground up. The political elites in the parties, government, organizations and corporations try to manage – that is, manipulate – the public sphere. Most often they succeed in doing so, according to Habermas. It is one-way communication rather than dialogue, and hence we can speak of a representative public. Politicians, state representatives and corporations use the public sphere as a means to generate legitimacy for their interests and policies; that is, they represent themselves before the public. The role of the citizens is reduced to that of acclaiming, or not, what they are presented with, whether in the voting booth, when shopping, or with the remote control. The best example of that today is no doubt that of spin and spin doctors, formerly known as public relations (ibid., 193). With the help of spin, politicians and corporations try to present themselves and events in a particular light in order to garner legitimacy for their cause. Public opinion is managed; indeed it is no longer a public but a 'nonpublic' (ibid., 211), because it has decomposed in both its audience and its common interest in reason.

It is a pretty bleak picture Habermas gives us of the public sphere in the mid-twentieth century Western world. Whether or not things have got worse is an open question. It is clear, however, that there is no way back to an earlier, more exclusive public sphere. Society is too complex, and given our subscription to principles of equality and inclusion, it would be unjust to exclude the masses.

What is the alternative then? Below, I shall consider how Habermas responds to criticisms that he was too pessimistic about the state of the public sphere, and I shall consider how he revises his solution. In *The Structural Transformation of the Public Sphere*, his solution is to argue for what is sometimes referred to as 'the long march through the institutions'. The idea is to use organized interest groups in a more positive fashion. Habermas (ibid., 210) writes:

Institutionalized in the mass democracy of the social-welfare state no differently than in the bourgeois constitutional state, the idea of publicity (at one time the rationalization of domination in the medium of the critical public debate of private people) is today realizable only as a rationalization – limited, of course, because of the plurality of organized private interests – of the exercise of societal and political power under the mutual control of rival organizations themselves committed to publicity as regards both their internal structure and their interaction with one another and with the state.

Thus, Habermas's solution is to take democratic associations and institutions as the building blocks of the public sphere, fostering rational-critical debate within them, among them and between them and the state. If properly democratized, these organizations would function as the channels for public reasoning and for demands from below. Although Habermas (ibid., 210) gives up on a public sphere made up of individual citizens, he sees some possibilities in the democratization of these organizations:

To be able to satisfy these functions in the sense of democratic opinion and consensus formation their inner structure must first be organized in accord with the principle of publicity and must institutionally permit an intraparty or intra-association democracy – to allow for unhampered communication and public rational-critical debate.

CRITIQUE I: HABERMAS'S IDEALIZATION OF
THE BOURGEOIS PUBLIC SPHERE

Given the attention paid to *The Structural Transformation of the Public Sphere*, first in Germany and then in the English speaking world, it can come as no surprise that the book elicited a wide range of criticisms. I want to focus on two clusters of criticism. In the following section, I examine the claim that Habermas was too pessimistic in his description of the contemporary public sphere, and I also describe how Habermas later redirected his account of the public sphere as part of his theory of deliberative democracy. In this section, I examine the claim that Habermas was too optimistic in his description of the bourgeois public sphere in its heyday. There are a number of criticisms that converge here. They converge around the claim that Habermas paid insufficient attention to the biases and exclusions in the bourgeois public sphere, and that he therefore idealized it. For instance, Habermas does not stress how, during the supposed golden age of the public sphere, the press *also* contained gossip, scandal, lurid stories and other things that were hardly conducive to the kind of rational debate that he is after.

A central point of critique is raised by feminist scholars. They argue that Habermas does not pay sufficient attention to the patriarchal structure of the public sphere. Habermas did not deny the patriarchal structure of the private sphere where the man was the head of the household. He also did not deny the limited, not to say non-existing, political and civil rights of women in the seventeenth, eighteenth and nineteenth centuries. What the critics claim, however, is that the public sphere was essentially patriarchal in nature. That is, the patriarchal structures in the rest of society spilled over into the public sphere, while the apparent disregard for differences in the public sphere merely hid this patriarchal bias. Although the bourgeois and the liberals would talk of humans, they could not really imagine a woman as that kind of reasoning human being. This is reflected in the vocabulary used at the time in the case of 'the rights of man', for instance.

What is more, even if these prejudices were overcome and women were included into the public sphere, they would still be in an unequal position, because the very structure of the public sphere was patriarchal. The argument is that the public sphere relies on a public/private distinction that is itself gendered. It relegates differences that are considered feminine to the private, and what is considered masculine is given a place in the public and considered universal and neutral (i.e. it is naturalized as 'human'). Thus, when women enter into the public sphere, they do so on terms that are masculine, and they do so as bearers of difference (whether related to bodies, sexuality, feelings or experiences). They are marked as women, and, as such, they are marked both as (hu)mans and as different from this supposedly universal and neutral category of '(hu)man'. Men, on the other hand, do not suffer from this bias because their identity is not counted as a difference; being a man is identical to being a human being.[3]

Habermas acknowledges the biases and exclusions in the public sphere, but he believes that they are not constitutive of the public sphere. That is, he believes that it is possible to overcome them through a process of immanent critique, where the biases and exclusions are held up against the promise of equality and inclusion that is inherent in the self-understanding of the public sphere from the very beginning (Habermas 1992a, 425–9). 'Bourgeois publicness', he writes,

> is articulated in discourses that provided areas of common ground not only for the labor movement but also for the excluded other, that is, the feminist movement. Contact with these movements in turn transformed these discourses and the structures of the public sphere from within. (Habermas 1989a, 429)

Thus, the patriarchal terrain of the public sphere is not left intact when new groups – including women – are included as equals within it. In short, the public sphere is not essentially masculine.

Another exclusion for which Habermas is criticized is the exclusion of the plebeian public sphere from consideration in *The Structural Transformation of the Public Sphere*. In the 'Author's Preface' to the book, Habermas (ibid., xviii) himself notes that he is focusing on the bourgeois or liberal public sphere and excludes the plebeian public sphere from consideration. His justification is that the plebeian public sphere must be understood as derivative of the bourgeois public sphere. This is so because we are dealing with bourgeois *society* and therefore all agents within that society will gravitate towards the dominant bourgeois institutions. Thus the plebs will tend to seek inclusion within the bourgeois public sphere, and whatever goes on in the plebeian public sphere must be seen as a precursor to this.

One problem with this is that, in this way, Habermas treats society and the public sphere as totalities. This holistic view ignores the differentiation and divisions within society and within the public sphere.[4] The consequence is that the state of the public sphere will be judged on the basis of what is in fact only one public sphere among others, namely the bourgeois/liberal one. Thereby Habermas also overlooks the potentials for radical politics in other parts of society. This is so not least in relation to the radical potential of the plebeian public sphere, where anarchists, communists and radicals played an important role in the struggle for equal rights and better conditions for the non-propertied classes.[5] Later, Habermas revised his view of the public sphere by accepting that there is not one public sphere, but many overlapping and conflicting public spheres. He refers to the 'pluralization of the public sphere' and 'competing public spheres' (Habermas 1992a, 426, 425; see also Fraser 1992; and Calhoun 1992b, 37f.).

CRITIQUE II: HABERMAS'S PESSIMISTIC VIEW OF THE STATE OF THE CONTEMPORARY PUBLIC SPHERE

Some commentators have criticized Habermas for a too simplistic and pessimistic account of the contemporary state of the public sphere, which is to say the public sphere of the 1950s. There are indeed places in *The Structural Transformation of the Public Sphere* where Habermas sounds more like Horkheimer and Adorno and their critique of the culture industry in *Dialectic of Enlightenment* (2002). There may be several reasons for Habermas's undue pessimism.

One reason is that Habermas overlooks the potential of non-bourgeois public spheres, such as the plebeian one. Thereby the decomposition of the bourgeois public sphere appears as the decomposition of the public sphere and of radical politics as such. If Habermas had paid more attention to alternative public spheres, the decline and disintegration of the bourgeois public sphere may not necessarily be such a loss if there were alternatives to it. The focus on the bourgeois public sphere specifically leads to a pessimistic view of the contemporary state of the public sphere.

Another reason for Habermas's pessimistic view may be that Habermas does not spend much energy on social movements, whether historical or contemporary (Calhoun 1992b, 36f.). This is linked to the point about alternative publics. Both historically and today, social movements often emerge from the bottom and from the fringes of society. Thus they may be imperceptible from a perspective that focuses on the bourgeois/liberal public sphere. This point is all the more important given developments after the initial publication of *The Structural Transformation of the Public Sphere* in 1962. Here I am thinking of the different social movements of the 1960s and 1970s – the student, peace, environmental, civil rights and women's movements – and the role that social movements played during and after the fall of Communism in Eastern Europe.

Part of Habermas's (1992a, 425f.) response to these points about his pessimism is to draw attention to alternative and competing publics and the potential in them. Likewise he acknowledges the role played by social movements during the last half century; thus, civil society plays an important part in his theory of deliberative democracy. But Habermas's reformulation of his theory of the public sphere is more fundamental than that because he makes it part of his theory of deliberative democracy, which he developed in the late 1980s and 1990s, especially in *Between Facts and Norms* (Habermas 1996a, chapter 8). He seeks to develop a more 'positive' role for the public spheres.

Habermas now places the public spheres at the beginning of a processual model of the political system. Following Nancy Fraser (1992, 89–92), Habermas speaks of 'weak' and 'strong' publics. Weak publics are found in civil society and they are characterized by opinion and identity formation. That is, citizens debate issues of the day and form opinions and collective and individual identities. Strong publics consist of, for instance, the public in parliament. Here opinion formation and decision making melt together. That is, the participants do not just debate and form opinions but also take decisions on the basis of those opinions.

Weak publics feed into strong publics. The 'wilder' publics of civil society are more sensitive to demands and pathologies in society, and they are better at generating communicative power, that is, power generated from action oriented towards mutual understanding. The conditions for this kind of practice are better in the informal networks of civil society. However, the opinions developed in the weak publics must be fed into the political system in order eventually to become law. In this way Habermas talks about the 'circulation' of communicative power, and the source of this circulation is the weak publics.

Thus, the public spheres are part of a wider deliberative democracy, and specifically they are the institutional setting for an important part of the deliberations of deliberative democracy (Habermas 1996a, chapter 8). More generally, the public spheres form part of Habermas's theories of communicative action and discourse ethics, which Habermas developed in the 1970s and 1980s, and which are the subjects of the following two chapters. Communicative action and (rational) discourse are aimed at mutual understanding that is not imposed but based on the forceless force of the better argument. Although not a blueprint for a future society, the theories of communicative action and rational discourse nonetheless point to a solution to the pathologies of contemporary society. They also point to a way to solve the problems associated with the bourgeois public sphere in its historical and contemporary forms. This is important. To conceive of the public sphere in this communicative form brings in a future-oriented perspective that locates the solution to any problems in the public spheres squarely in a future 'communicative' overcoming of those problems. The solution to the problems with the public spheres lies in better communication, that is, better conditions for participants to engage in a domination-free, rational dialogue.

There is one important qualification to this, however. Habermas does not believe that communicative action can penetrate society as a whole. Society is too complex for that. That is why he insists on a distinction between systems and lifeworld, as we shall see in the following chapter. Systems are organized on the basis of the steering media money and power, for instance, in the market and in the state. The lifeworld is integrated through the medium of communicative action. In relation to the public spheres, the point is that, while the public spheres have an important role to play in deliberative democracy, some things must be left to the systems. Not everything can be the subject of rational deliberation and consensus formation in the public spheres all the time.

This limits the role of the public spheres. Habermas conceived of this limitation in different ways. At first, he believes that we must build a bulwark against the systems:

> The goal is no longer to supersede an economic system having a capitalist life of its own and a system of domination having a bureaucratic life of its own but to erect a democratic dam against

the colonizing *encroachment* of system imperatives on areas of the lifeworld. (Habermas 1992a, 444)

Thus, the idea is to build a dam to protect the communicative action of the lifeworld – for instance, in the public spheres – against the systems, that is, the market and the state. Later, however, Habermas believes that it is possible to attach the systems to the lifeworld by making the law dependent on communicative action. This is the argument he develops in *Between Facts and Norms*. The public sphere thus becomes the course of the legitimacy of the law; citizens must first have deliberated freely and equally and in this way have formed their opinions, and this is then fed into the political system via the strong publics in, for instance, the parliament (Habermas 1996a, 359ff.). This is the subject of Chapter 5.

THE PUBLIC SPHERE IN PRACTICE: STUDENT PROTESTS

As mentioned earlier, Habermas has made numerous interventions in the public sphere as a public intellectual. His interventions in the debates about students, politics and the university in the 1960s also testify to this. Before publishing *The Structural Transformation of the Public Sphere*, Habermas co-authored a study of the political mentality of West German university students, *Student und Politik (Student and Politics)* (Habermas et al. 1961). The study showed that West German students were not democratically minded in the late 1950s, but rather had an authoritarian view of politics. Later, however, the student movement of the 1960s showed that German students were often just as radical as their counterparts in, for instance, France and the United States. Initially the debates in and around the West German universities concerned the structure of the universities, but later they took on a more general societal focus. Here I shall focus on the debates about the university structure.

With respect to those debates, Habermas sought to find a way to avoid, on the one hand, useless talks between professors/administration and the students with no real influence for the latter; and, on the other hand, what Habermas (1981, 232f., 304ff.) referred to as some students' 'pure actionism', that is, a fetishism of action – action for the sake of action.[6] The inclusion of the voice of the students in the organization of the university simply meant that the voices of the students were absorbed in the established system without any real potential for influence or change. However, according to Habermas, the fetishism of action was equally impotent because it only sought to oppose the established system without formulating any positive programme for change. What is more, the fetishism of action had irrational implications since it implied an aestheticization of action and violence that could not be rationally grounded in the public, but was, rather, subject to subjective whims. This is why Habermas at one point referred to it as 'playing with terror (with Fascist implications)' and as '"leftist Fascism"', formulations that he later regretted (ibid., 213, 214, 215).

For Habermas, political action should be viewed as partaking in public argumentation, that is, political action is analogous to argumentation. Arguments must be subject to intersubjective testing, for instance in the public sphere, which aesthetic expressions are not because they are ultimately subjective. The reasons that we can give for aesthetic judgements are at least partly confined by the first person perspective ('I like', and so on). Therefore they are to some extent inaccessible to intersubjective testing in the public sphere. This is what is behind Habermas's assertion that the 'actionistic' parts of the student movement have become susceptible to 'irrational impulses'. 'They are no longer willing to commit themselves to the claim to rationality of discussions', he believed (ibid., 265f.). Likewise, for Habermas, the aim of the student movement ought to be that decisions taken within the university should be taken through public deliberation with access for all those concerned, irrespective of their status in society (as professors or students, for instance). According to Habermas (ibid., 283), public deliberation and the principles underlying it are the media through which everything else can be contested (say, the present system of laws), but stepping outside of public deliberation leads directly to 'irrationalism'.

Habermas attempts to find a way to mediate between, on the one hand, the existing system and institutions and, on the other hand, political action to change the system. This is also so in his writings on the public sphere where he is looking for radical changes to the bourgeois public sphere, but also commits to ideas inherent to the public sphere. In his writings on the student protests, Habermas stresses the use of two different media mediating the existing system and attempts to change it.

First, he underlines the importance of formal rules, which here refer to the rule of law and more generally to the (constitutional) principles underlying constitutional democracy. Formal rules are not necessarily impotent, according to Habermas; what is important is to give them material content, an argument he also uses against the more radical and Marxist critics of the bourgeois public sphere. Thus, warning against a forced loyalty towards the system, Habermas insists that we must avoid fetishizing existing rules even if we should not dismiss the essence of these rules. The essence of these rules refers to the principles underlying the liberal democratic order, including the rule of law, but these rules are subject to rational-critical debate. Habermas places one foot in the liberal democratic camp by emphasizing the importance of the rule of law and other principles, and another foot outside the existing order by emphasizing that the existing system can be criticized from the point of view of the very principles that it claims to realize, namely principles of equality, freedom and democracy. This is an example of immanent critique. He also refers to it as 'radical reformism' (ibid., 302).

Second, Habermas emphasizes the role of what he calls 'demonstrative violence', referring to demonstrations, happenings and so on, that serve to bring attention to arguments, and that he opposes to violence and vandalism in the traditional sense of these terms.[7] Argumentation is the second of the two central media for mediating institutions and action (alongside the principles of constitutional democracy), and other means must be judged and justified in relation to argumentation and the principles of constitutional democracy. Habermas opens the door for non-argumentative means, but these must be auxiliary and secondary to the public use of reason (as opposed to, for instance, the 'actionistic' part of the student protests, which were, according to Habermas, action for the sake of action). Against conservatives and authoritarians, Habermas underlines that formal rules and argumentation must leave room for and presuppose a certain maturity of the people (here, the students), which in turn needs room to develop. The participants in public argumentation must be given some leeway to experiment and to learn through trial and error. Argumentation is precisely seen by Habermas as a learning process among participants among whom no one can claim to know *the* correct outcome. The condition of learning in this case is that you leave the safe ground of the existing order behind. This is the kind of maturity characteristic of modernity and the Enlightenment that Kant (1991a) was referring to when he encouraged his contemporaries to use their own reason rather than rely on traditional authorities.

It should be clear by now how Habermas's conception of the public sphere informs his views of the student movement as a movement that both takes advantage of the public sphere (within and outside the universities) and seeks to radically reform the public sphere. It is also important to note the criticism that was put forward against Habermas's position. Although Habermas accepted what he calls 'demonstrative violence' in certain situations, there were those in the student movement and on the Left who criticized Habermas for being unduly conservative. Their point was that Habermas accepted too much of the existing capitalist society and bourgeois public sphere. He was not tolerant enough of the kind of tactics pursued by the students, and thereby he in fact reifies the dominant structures and prevents the social change that he is himself in favour of.[8] More generally, we can say that perhaps Habermas was unduly intolerant of the ways in which new constituencies (here, the students) tried to break into the public sphere in order to change it and tried to establish alternative public spheres. For instance, the 'actionistic' acts by the students were for the sake of interrupting present institutions, and as such they easily appear illegitimate from the perspective of those existing institutions, here the bourgeois public sphere. This is the recurring problem that Habermas faces: how to negotiate between the ideal of the public sphere and the biases and exclusions of the existing public spheres?

FURTHER READINGS

Habermas's writings on the public sphere are in *The Structural Transformation of the Public Sphere* (1989a), in *Between Facts and Norms* (1996a, chapter 8) and in two pieces in Craig Calhoun's (1992a) edited volume, *Habermas and the Public Sphere* ('Further Reflections on the Public Sphere' and 'Concluding Remarks', of which the former is particularly useful as it summarizes the argument of the original argument as well as the later changes to it). Although the contributions are of a varied quality and difficulty, Calhoun's (1992a) volume is easily the best collection of essays on Habermas's theory of the public sphere. Seyla Benhabib's (1992) contribution to the volume usefully sets out the differences between Habermas's theory of the public sphere and competing republican and liberal approaches. For a post-structuralist alternative view to Habermas, see Mouffe's piece, 'For an agonistic public sphere' (2005). Jean Cohen and Andrew Arato's (1992) *Civil Society and Political Theory* gives an extended overview of theories of civil society and the role of the public sphere therein from a perspective that is close to that of Habermas. James Bohman's (2000) *Public Deliberation* connects the public sphere to the theory of deliberative democracy, again from a perspective sympathetic to Habermas. Finally Robert Holub's (1991) book *Jürgen Habermas: Critic in the Public Sphere* is an excellent introduction to Habermas's engagement in academic and political public debates.

CHAPTER THREE

COMMUNICATIVE ACTION AND REASON

INTRODUCTION

In this chapter, I explain the basics of Habermas's theory of communicative action and reason. He developed this theory during the 1970s, first through writings on language theory, including speech act theory, and later in the monumental *The Theory of Communicative Action* (1984; 1987a; see also 1998a; 2001a) published in German in 1981. The book, which is divided into two volumes, clogs up 1,100 pages in the German original, a 'mere' 900 in the English translation. It is rightly seen as one of Habermas's main works, if not *the* main work, and it has been the subject of a large volume of secondary literature (Honneth and Joas 1991; Honneth et al. 1992; Ingram 1987).

Given the length of *The Theory of Communicative Action*, in addition to Habermas's other writings on the subject, and given the often detailed and technical discussion of other theorists and of theoretical points in sociological and linguistic theory, this chapter will have to limit itself to the basics of Habermas's theory. I shall have to pass over many of the finer points of the way Habermas develops the theory of communicative action and reason and of the distinctions and concepts he develops.

The length and detailed character of Habermas's work is due in part to the way he works, something that is especially visible in *The Theory of Communicative Action*. The book is at once a sociological and a philosophical work in that it attempts to combine a theory of action and language (sociology) with a theory of rationality (philosophy). It is clearly systematic in intent: Habermas wants to develop a theory of modern society and its pathologies. He seeks to develop a diagnosis and critique of contemporary society, but one that is both systematic and falsifiable through conceptual and empirical research. When Habermas works, he works his way through other theorists who have attempted answers to the questions he is interested in. In *The Theory of Communicative Action*, the central question is how modernity can develop a notion of reason without founding it in religion, and so on. In short, Habermas wants to develop a post-metaphysical theory of action and rationality. The question is whether there is a rational kernel to modernity, a rational kernel that we can dig out and use as a basis for a critique of the pathologies of modern societies.

In *The Theory of Communicative Action*, Habermas engages with Karl Marx, George Herbert Mead, Émile Durkheim, Max Weber, Georg Lukács and Talcott Parsons. 'I treat Weber, Mead, Durkheim, and Parsons as classics', he writes, 'that is, as theorists of society who still have something to say to us' (Habermas 1984, xlii). Habermas does not discuss these thinkers in order to simply reject or celebrate their positions, but rather in order to appropriate the parts that – from Habermas's perspective – are still valid and can help us understand contemporary society. It is, thus, an exercise in immanent critique. But notice also that Habermas develops his own perspective (the theory of communicative action and reason) through this critical appropriation of other thinkers. Habermas's way of working and writing makes the task all the more difficult for the reader because she must both understand Habermas's own theory and understand how Habermas appropriates and criticizes other thinkers. (Due to the limitations of space, I shall not summarize Habermas's discussions of other theorists.)

I start by explaining how Habermas bases his theory of communicative action and reason in language theory, specifically in speech act theory. I then briefly explain the main concepts and distinctions of the theory of communicative action and reason, after which I explain in some more detail how the system/lifeworld distinction forms the centre of Habermas's theory of modernity and contemporary society. Next I explain how the system/lifeworld distinction gives rise to the so-called colonization thesis, which forms the basis for Habermas's critique of the way markets and the state undermine communicative action and reason. I conclude by looking at what Habermas thinks needs to be done in response to the colonization of the lifeworld. Throughout the different sections, I shall present some of the main criticisms that have been raised against Habermas.

FORMAL PRAGMATICS

The intersubjectivist turn

Recall Habermas's argument for a shift from what he calls the philosophy of the subject (or of consciousness) to an intersubjectivist approach.[1] The philosophy of the subject is problematic for a number of reasons. In the context of the present chapter, the problem is that the philosophy of the subject is inherently linked to instrumental reason because it can only conceive of relations as relations between a subject and an object, whether the object is a thing or a person. This may not be a problem with regard to our relations to nature (although some environmentalist may argue the opposite). In our relation to nature, it is a matter of controlling nature for instrumental purposes (to build a house, to get something to eat, to develop new medicines and so on).

In the context of social relations, the picture is different, however. There the philosophy of the subject leads agents to treat other agents as objects, that is, as means to an end rather than as ends in themselves, to use the Kantian phrase. Other people become objects to be controlled and manipulated for my ends. Rationality is reduced to instrumental reason where it is a matter of the efficiency of means relative to a given end (How can I get others to do what I need them to do in order to further my own ends?). Seen in this light, it is no wonder that Max Weber sees modern reason as an iron cage: rationalization may secure material progress (including an efficient bureaucracy), but it also leads to disenchantment and alienation from other people. Similarly, Horkheimer and Adorno are only able to see emancipation through rationalization as in fact a new kind of bondage.

Habermas's purpose with the theory of communicative action and reason is to argue for a way out of this paradox while not giving up on reason. He argues that, because they are still wedded to the philosophy of consciousness, Weber, and Horkheimer and Adorno conceive of action and reason in a one-dimensional way, and so they cannot see how rationalization can also be emancipatory. Formal pragmatics is the first step in the development of the theory of communicative action and reason, because it is with the formal pragmatics that Habermas develops his intersubjectivist approach.[2] The latter is based in a theory of language, which is expressed in the

'Appendix' to *Knowledge and Human Interests*, quoted above in Chapter 1: 'What raises us out of nature is the only thing whose nature we can know: language. Through its structure, autonomy and responsibility are posited for us. Our first sentence expresses unequivocally the intention of universal and unconstrained consensus' (Habermas 1987b, 314). In language and communication, Habermas finds a source of reason, and hence emancipation, that is not transcendental in the traditional sense (like God or Nature), but 'quasi-transcendental', because it is based in ordinary language, that is, in our everyday communication.

Rational reconstruction

In developing his theory of communicative action and reason, Habermas uses what he calls a 'rational reconstructive' method. Formal pragmatics is an example of a rational reconstructive method. It 'focuses on the general and necessary conditions for the validity of symbolic expressions and achievements' (Habermas 1990, 31; see also 1998a, chapter 1). Habermas's focus is on how we can generate rational answers to practical questions in an intersubjective fashion and under post-metaphysical and post-traditional conditions.

Rational reconstructions combine philosophy with science, that is, abstract and conceptual theorizing with empirical theories of society and language, for instance. Philosophy and reconstructive empirical sciences are supposed to work hand in hand, with one checking the always fallible results of the other. On the one hand, this combination of philosophy and science is supposed to avoid an empiricism that provides no critical distance from ourselves; on the other hand, this combination is supposed to avoid a stronger transcendentalism that relies on privileged insight into a transcendental realm. In Habermas's (2002, 91) own words, he tries 'to steer between the Scylla of a levelling, transcendence-less empiricism and the Charybdis of a high-flying idealism that glorifies'. With this combination of philosophy and empirical science, of transcendence and empiricism, Habermas refers to the universal structures he reconstructs as quasi-transcendental.

There is always the danger that we take something to be truly universal, which is not actually so (for instance, if we take a particular trait of a particular language to be universal). Therefore Habermas refers to the reconstructed universals as fallible and hypothetical. He writes:

> [A]ll rational reconstructions, like other types of knowledge, have only hypothetical status. There is always the possibility that they rest on a false choice of examples, that they are obscuring and distorting correct intuitions, or, more frequently, that they are overgeneralizing individual cases. (Habermas 1990, 32)

Although the rational reconstructions may be universal, they are also fallible and we must always be able to test their universality again.

Habermas thinks of the rational reconstructions – and, so, of formal pragmatics – in terms of science and knowledge. This makes him able to locate reason and emancipation and a kind of utopian energy in facts about language and social action. Furthermore, although the structures he reconstructs should be treated as fallible, they are supposed to be universal (hence the reason why he used to refer to formal pragmatics as 'universal pragmatics'). Thus, there is a universalistic and systematic intent behind formal pragmatics. Habermas is reconstructing the communicative competences that are common to all languages and language users. That is, he tries to reconstruct what makes us able to engage in communication irrespective of where we are from or which language we use. In this he can be distinguished from someone like Ludwig Wittgenstein (1958) who was also interested in the pragmatic aspects of language and the competences necessary for using language. However, Wittgenstein thought of these competences as specific to particular language games and forms of life; for Habermas, this creates a danger of relativism. Habermas (1998a, 52–62), then, is interested in what different language games have in common – in what is *universal* to them. Importantly, for Habermas, the universal structures he reconstructs are not just empirical facts, but have a normative force as well.

Speech act theory

As mentioned above, Habermas draws on a wealth of linguistic and social theories, which he discusses and appropriates for his own purposes. It is not necessary to know the details of the way in which he appropriates linguistic theory for his formal pragmatics, but some of the concepts and distinctions are important.

An important source of inspiration for Habermas is speech act theory, especially as developed by J. L. Austin (1975) and John Searle (1969). Speech act theory comes out of the Anglo-Saxon tradition of analytical philosophy, but speech act theorists are interested in ordinary language rather than logic. In addition, Austin and Searle do not reduce language to reference or truth to correspondence with a reality outside language. Rather, they view language as part of social action and reality – hence the title of Austin's book: *How to Do Things with Words* (1975). This is why Habermas is interested in speech act theory because he is interested in the pragmatics of language, that is, in how language is used by real life agents, and how we can do something *in* speaking. For instance, language is not only used to refer to things in the world ('now my computer broke down again'), but also in ways that cannot be characterized as referring, but rather as doing (for instance when I say 'welcome' to someone).

Austin makes some important distinctions, which Habermas (1998a, 66–88; 1984, 288–95) takes on board. They are distinctions between different aspects of linguistic utterances (i.e. sentences): locutionary, illocutionary and perlocutionary. The locutionary aspect of utterances refers to something in the world or, more technically, expresses a state of affairs (for instance, 'I am a professor'). The illocutionary aspect of utterances refers to what we do *in* saying something; for instance, if I say 'I promise to be on time next week', then I am doing something (promising) in saying something ('I promise . . .'). Finally, the perlocutionary aspect refers to what we do *through*, or *by*, saying something; for instance, I might achieve a certain effect by threatening you: 'if you don't come on time, I won't wait for you'. Habermas is particularly interested in the illocutionary aspect, because he believes that it contains the seeds for establishing a normative relationship between two or more speakers. In addition, unlike Austin, Habermas is particularly interested in those speech acts that are not already governed by conventions, because he is interested in the way in which speech acts can be the source for conventions, especially norms.

Take now the following example of a speech act: 'I promise to hand in my essay tomorrow by 4 o'clock'. This speech act could be said to establish a normative relationship between a student and a professor by establishing certain normative expectations. The speech act has a locutionary aspect insofar as it expresses a state of affairs (about an essay, time and so on). It also has an illocutionary aspect: in saying this, the student is making a promise. And, finally, the speech act has a perlocutionary aspect: the student may be trying to get an extension to the essay deadline or to avoid getting a penalty on the late essay. As far as the perlocutionary aspect goes, the intentions of the speakers can be hidden from the hearer. For instance, the professor does not need to know what the student wants to achieve (or achieves) in order for the speech act to be successful (or felicitous, in Austin's term). The student may achieve his goal of avoiding a penalty even if he does not tell the professor that this is his goal. Notice that the perlocutionary involves a purpose, and later Habermas links this aspect of language to purposeful action and to strategic rationality.

As far as the illocutionary aspect goes, however, the speech act must be transparent, because it only works if the other understands my intentions. In our example, the promise only works as a promise if both the student and the professor understand it as such. There must be mutual understanding; if there is not, then communication breaks down. Later Habermas links this aspect of language to communicative action, which is action oriented towards mutual understanding. For Habermas, the illocutionary aspect of language enjoys primacy. In order to use language in the perlocutionary or purpose-oriented way, we must master language in the illocutionary sense, he argues, because we must be able to communicate meaning to others (Habermas 1984, 288f.). This is very important, because Habermas wants to locate a normative force (reason and emancipation) in language and specifically in the illocutionary aspect of language use. In addition, he wants to show that this normative force is universal and necessary and is not something we can choose. That is, he wants to show that we cannot but orient ourselves towards mutual understanding when we communicate; or, by virtue of the very structure of language, we are aiming towards consensus. So, even if the student in our example may simply be seeking a certain (perlocutionary) effect with her speech act, she cannot avoid *also* orienting herself towards mutual understanding. The illocutionary aspect of speech acts enjoys primacy, and so does communicative action.

Before moving on to the way Habermas links speech act theory to an account of different validity claims, I will mention three (partly related) criticisms of the way he proceeds with speech act theory.

First, following Austin, Habermas focuses on serious speech acts and differentiates these from the beginning. The theory of communicative action and reason is based on an analysis of serious speech acts.

This, it may be argued, limits the scope of the theory to only serious uses of language, whereas other uses of language – aesthetic and humoristic ones, for example – are unaccounted for. What, we may ask, about the role of aesthetic expressions and humour in communication? Even in the cases where we use language in an illocutionary fashion, these uses of language can have an important role to play. Habermas prioritizes the problem solving function of language over language as world-disclosure, that is, the ability of language to 'open up' the world for us, which is central to aesthetic expression. Because Habermas prioritizes the problem solving function of language, he needs to distinguish those forms of language where language works as a transparent medium for one's intentions. Thus, the focus on problem solving (e.g. establishing normative relationships) means that certain uses of language are rendered secondary, which, it may be argued, are actually very important for communication.

Second, as mentioned, Habermas believes that language and meanings can, at least in theory, be transparent so that my intentions can be understood by the other and we can achieve a mutual understanding. This idea of the transparency of language is open to a critique that Jacques Derrida (1988; see Habermas 1987c) has put forward against Austin and Searle. Derrida's point is that language is inherently opaque. Meaning is never stable, and we cannot control how utterances are taken up (i.e. understood) by others. Thus, no matter how much back and forth communication takes place between the student and the professor, they can never be one hundred percent certain that they have achieved mutual understanding and that they have understood the other's intentions. What is more, opacity is what makes communication possible. If there were transparency, we would quickly run out of things to talk about. Likewise with disagreement. Habermas takes mutual agreement and consensus as signs of rationality, but if we achieve a transparent consensus, then there would be no need for further communication. Thus, we need opacity and disagreement for communication to be meaningful (Derrida 1988; Thomassen 2007, 27–33).

Third, and finally, Habermas uses the illocutionary/perlocutionary distinction to distinguish communication oriented at mutual understanding (illocutionary) from communication oriented at achieving a purpose (perlocutionary). However, as Culler argues, this rests on a misunderstanding of speech act theory because illocutionary speech acts are also aimed at achieving a purpose or a goal, for instance

making a promise or, more abstractly, establishing a normative relationship. Thus, the illocutionary use of language is also teleological,
and the two kinds of communication cannot be distinguished so
easily (Culler 1985, especially 137). This critique is linked to the critique that Habermas idealizes communicative action, and that it is
not possible to distinguish communicative action from power. I shall
return to this critique below.

Speech acts and validity

I now turn to explain how Habermas links speech act theory to an
account of validity. Every speech act aimed at mutual understanding
contains three validity claims, although often one of them will be
dominant in any particular speech act. The three validity claims are
claims to truth, normative rightness and truthfulness or authenticity.[3] Each of these claims are linked to relations to different 'worlds':
the external, objective world (truth), the intersubjective, social world
(rightness) and the internal, subjective world (truthfulness). Habermas
also talks about three formal pragmatic functions of language: a cognitive, an interactive and an expressive function. These functions
correspond to the three validity claims that I make when speaking,
namely to represent something in the world (truth), to establish legitimate intersubjective relations (rightness) and to express my intentions (truthfulness). In this way, Habermas connects validity claims,
relations to different aspects of the world and functions of language
(Habermas 1984, 75ff.). Often speech acts go unchallenged, and language and action take place against a shared and implicit background,
which Habermas calls the lifeworld. But if the validity claims are
contested, then the agents can shift to discourse (or what Habermas
also calls argumentation), where they deliberate their disagreements
and seek to arrive at a mutual agreement (ibid., 18).

With these distinctions in mind, recall now the earlier example
with the professor and the student. The student says to the professor:
'I promise to hand in my essay tomorrow by 4 o'clock'.[4] This speech
act contains claims to truth, rightness and truthfulness. The student
makes a claim to truth, a claim about the objective world: it is the
case that he will hand in an essay tomorrow. He also makes a claim
about the right norms that should govern the situation. Imagine, for
example, that the deadline for handing in the essay was today; in that
case, the student is making an implicit claim about the rightness of

asking one's professor for an extension to the deadline when he promises to hand in the essay tomorrow. Finally, the student is making a claim to truthfully represent his intentions, effectively claiming that he is not lying and really does intent to hand in the essay tomorrow by the promised time. In this example, we may say that the dominant validity claim is the one to truthfulness ('I promise . . .', that is, 'I really intent to . . .'), although all three validity claims are present.

All of the validity claims may be challenged. For instance, the professor may respond that tomorrow is a public holiday and so the university will be closed, so as a matter of fact the student cannot possibly hand in the essay. She might also respond that everybody else has handed in their essays by the deadline today, and that this is the norm in these situations, which is only fair because it treats everybody in the same way. Finally, the professor may point out that the student has previously made promises of this sort without delivering on those promises, so past discrepancies between promises and action suggests that the student does not really mean what he says. Of course, the student can then reply in different ways (for instance, 'my uncle just died, so you must make an exception to the norm in order to treat me equally with the others').

The validity of the validity claims may be tested in different ways. The claims to truth may be tested through discourse, where the agents deliberate about the truth of the matter, and through references to evidence (in our example, pointing to the university calendar, for example). Normative rightness may be tested through discourse about what the norm ought to be, that is, what we can expect of one another (e.g. about handing in essays by deadlines that are the same for everybody). Finally, truthfulness can be tested by comparing utterances with actions; this can only be done after the fact, although previous experiences may serve as evidence as we saw in our example with the student who has consistently broken his promises to the professor.

COMMUNICATIVE ACTION AND REASON

With these concepts and distinctions, we can now move on to look at the notions of communicative action and reason. Here I shall merely present the basic concepts and distinctions, and we shall see how Habermas translates the insights from linguistic theory into a theory of action and reason.

Habermas distinguishes between different types, or models, of action: the teleological, the norm guided, the dramaturgical and the communicative.[5] Teleological action is aimed at the objective world vis-à-vis which one relates either cognitively or volitionally, seeking either truth or effectiveness. Teleological action can be non-social, in which case it is guided by instrumental rationality, or social, in which case it is guided by strategic rationality. Norm guided action is aimed at the social, intersubjective world, and here it is a matter of normative rightness or legitimacy; this type of action is assessed according to normative expectations. Dramaturgical action is related to the subjective world, and is guided and assessed by the criteria of truthfulness (whether I am trying to deceive others) and authenticity (whether I suffer from self-deception). These three types of action corresponds easily to the three kinds of validity claims, relations to aspects of the world and functions of language.

In the communicative model of action, which is action oriented towards mutual understanding, agents are presumed to be able to relate to all three aspects of the world and to all three validity claims at the same time. Consequently, communicative action can be assessed according to all three criteria of truth, rightness and truthfulness/authenticity. It is important to highlight the essential difference between communicative and instrumental/strategic action. Where the latter are oriented towards success in the non-social and social worlds respectively, the former is oriented towards reaching understanding in the social world (ibid., 285–8). This difference is central to much of Habermas's theoretical framework, and I shall return to it later.

In the case of communicative action, action and language are intrinsically linked. In order to understand a communicative speech act, one must know what makes it acceptable (or could make it acceptable); that is, in order to understand the speech act, one must be able to see what makes it acceptable for the speaker. What this means is that an interpreter must be able to see the reasons with which one might defend the validity claims raised by the speech act. Habermas (ibid., 297f.) writes:

We understand a speech act when we know what makes it acceptable. From the standpoint of the speaker, the conditions of acceptability are identical to the conditions for his illocutionary success.

Acceptability is not defined here in an objectivistic sense, from the perspective of an observer, but in the performative attitude of a participant in communication.

It is not a matter, then, of whether I know what the dominant norms are. Although this may be important for me in navigating the social situation, more is needed for understanding a speech act and its validity claims in the sense of understanding that Habermas has in mind here. It is not enough for the professor in our example to know what the norms regulating submission of essays in her university are. Rather, understanding proceeds in what Habermas here refers to as a 'performative' mode. What this means is that it is mutual understanding, where I am able to understand the reasons that the other may give for her validity claims and to understand why these may be good reasons. To be more precise, I am forced to take a position on the validity claims and, thus, become involved in reasoning (ibid., 115f.). It starts with a validity claim, and this validity claim also contains the wager that, if challenged, I will be able to give reasons for it, and I will be ready to do so in a discourse that is free from power, characterized by symmetry and full information and so on. Thus, both the speaker and the hearer become embroiled in reasoning – in giving reasons for validity claims, and they implicitly assume that, if they had to, they would be able to defend their reasons and validity claims under conditions where only the better argument counts. Rationality is, in a sense, located in this wager to defend one's validity claims with reasons, and with reasons only, if challenged to do so. We need not actually engage in this sort of rational discourse, but it must at least be counterfactually assumed.

There is a movement from communicative action, to discourse and rational discourse. Communicative action takes place against the implicit background consensus of the lifeworld, where norms, and so on, are taken as given. We are always already situated within this mostly unquestioned lifeworld consensus (Habermas 1987a, 119ff.). Communicative action complements the lifeworld in the sense that the lifeworld can only be reproduced through communicative action, as opposed to instrumental or strategic action (Habermas 1984, 337).

If the validity claims of a communicative speech act are challenged, then we can move to discourse (or argumentation) where 'participants thematize contested validity claims and attempt to vindicate or criticize them through arguments' (ibid., 18). A validity claim is always put forward in a particular lifeworld context, but at the same time it points beyond that context to the possibility that it may be vindicated in discourse in 'ever wider forums before an ever more competent and larger audience against ever new objections' (Habermas 2001c, 36). If the discourse meets certain criteria, we have a rational discourse. Those criteria include the full and equal inclusion of everybody affected, that only the forceless force of the better argument maters, and that the discourse participants are sincere. There can be no internal or external constraints on the deliberations in a rational discourse, 'only the unforced force of the better argument' is supposed to count (Habermas 1993, 163).[6] The outcome of such a rational discourse will be a rational consensus 'to which all possibly affected persons could assent as participants in rational discourse' (Habermas 1996a, 107). Habermas translates these points into a discourse ethics and a theory of deliberative democracy. I shall return to these in the next two chapters, where I shall also explain the notions of discourse and consensus more fully.

Note that, in this way, rational consensus is intrinsically linked to communicative action, albeit only in the weak sense of counterfactual '*idealizing suppositions* we cannot avoid making' (Habermas 2001c, 13). Rational consensus and rational discourse function both as a regulative idea (because they are facts of reason that give communication a certain telos) and as critical ideals, even if only conceived as a counterfactual: they are '*actually effective* in ways that point beyond the limits of actual situations' (ibid.). Indeed, they are 'idealizing presuppositions' rather than ideals. Importantly, and as opposed to Kant, the idea(l) is a 'detranscendentalized' and 'immanentized' one. Habermas (ibid., 15) writes that 'the sharp clarity of Kant's oppositions (constitutive vs. regulative, transcendental vs. empirical, immanent vs. transcendent, etc.) diminishes', because we are no longer dealing with a monological subject but with the reason built into social practices of communicative action.

This is the way in which Habermas attempts to situate critical theory in a theory of language and action, thus situating a critical force in the very fact that, as human beings, we are linguistic and communicating beings. Here is the link between action, language and rationality. And here is the link between the quote from the 'Appendix' to *Knowledge and Human Interests* to *The Theory of*

Communicative Action, and beyond that to Habermas's discourse ethics and theory of deliberative democracy. The next step is to translate these insights into a critical theory of contemporary society. To do so, Habermas develops the notions of lifeworld and system. But before looking at these in the next section, it is necessary to consider one final issue in relation to the argument for communicative action and reason.

Habermas believes that, without an account of communicative action and reason, it is impossible to explain how societies can be integrated peacefully in the long run, that is to say, in a way that does not rest on manipulation and violence. Some of Habermas's critics have argued that manipulation and violence are characteristics of all hitherto existing societies, and that it is impossible to have a society without manipulation and violence. Habermas does not deny the existence of manipulation and violence – and of instrumental and strategic action – and the point of his critical theory of society is to identify to these phenomena in contemporary society.

However, Habermas believes that it is necessary to distinguish between communicative and instrumental/strategic action and rationality, and that it is necessary to isolate the former from the latter. Only if we do so, is it possible to pull ourselves above the fray of manipulation and violence and criticize these. Only if we have established a point that is free from manipulation and violence (namely communicative action and reason), can our critique of these phenomena claim to be not just another exercise of manipulation and violence. If everything is reduced to power, then the critique of power can only be yet another instance of power. This is precisely Habermas's problem with Horkheimer and Adorno's (in his view) total critique of reason: they do not leave us with any account of reason from which to criticize degenerated forms of reason.

Habermas's notion of communicative reason is supposed to solve this problem. Indeed, Habermas's argument is that if Horkheimer and Adorno's argument about reason is to be an argument at all, they must at least implicitly assume something like communicative reason. If they did not, they would become embroiled in a performative contradiction where they would be saying one thing ('reason is power') while doing another (reasoning with the purpose of convincing us with good reasons). Thus, Habermas believes that communicative action and reason are not things that we can, in the long run, choose; they are given to us by the very fact that we are social beings.

LIFEWORLD AND SYSTEMS

In the introduction to this chapter, I mentioned that, with the theory of communicative action and reason, Habermas seeks a solution to a paradox of modernity or rationality: on the one hand, modernity can be described as an increase in rationality; on the other hand, rationalization reduces life to a matter of efficiency, thus appearing as a loss. Take, for example, the practice of getting a loan from your bank. Today, I do not need to befriend the bank manager or be related to him or have a certain status within society in order to get a loan from the bank. All that is needed is that I meet certain pre-established criteria about liquidity, income, and so on, and the bank then calculates whether it is worth taking the risk to lend me the money. This is a more egalitarian way of lending and borrowing money, and it is more efficient for society as a whole. But it also involves a loss. It may well be that I feel alienated from the whole lending process, which appears removed from my lifeworld and from the particularities of my situation ('why can't they see that I really need this loan?', and so on). And it may well be that the process makes me feel alienated from other agents: I can do the application for a loan from my computer at home, which is more efficient, but I also lose the opportunity to have a chat with the bank advisor, an old friend of the family.

This example is only one among many similar, and often more serious, examples. How does Habermas make sense of this kind of phenomena and of the paradox of rationalization? He does so with the concepts of lifeworld and system, which he links to a conception of modernity as rationalization (Habermas 1987a, chapter 6).

The lifeworld is, as mentioned above, the implicit background horizon or consensus for communicative action. The lifeworld and communicative action (understood as the symbolic reproduction of the lifeworld) are complementary concepts. The lifeworld is reproduced through communicative action, and it can be challenged in the way described in the previous section, but only bit by bit and not all at once. Thus, it is not a static conception of the lifeworld; it changes over time. The lifeworld consists of different structural components: culture, society and personality. In culture, you have cultural reproduction; in society, social integration; and in personality, socialization. Habermas (ibid., 137f.) writes about the complementary functions of communicative action:

> Under the functional aspect of *mutual understanding*, communicative action serves to transmit and renew cultural knowledge; under the aspect of *coordinating action*, it serves social integration and the establishment of solidarity; finally, under the aspect of *socialization*, communicative action serves the formation of personal identities. . . . Corresponding to these processes of *cultural reproduction*, *social integration*, and *socialization* are the structural components of the lifeworld: culture, society, person.

Modernity can be understood as two simultaneous differentiation processes, which can in turn be understood as processes of rationalization.[7] There is first the internal differentiation of the lifeworld into its different structural components: culture, society and personality. We are no longer defined by particular roles, and we can occupy more than one role. Roles are open to negotiation, and we are not born into them. I can become a colonel in the military even if I was born into a working class family, for instance. At the same time, norms become more abstract and are not so closely tied to particular situations. Norms become more formal and universal. In abstract terms, there is an increasing distinction between form and content of norms as well as increasing levels of reflexivity. These developments all have an emancipatory (and egalitarian) potential, and so we can talk about the rationalization of the lifeworld. Habermas also links this rationalization to the development of a 'post-conventional' consciousness, where agents do not need to fall back on conventions (i.e. existing norms and traditions), but relate critically to these. I return to this in the following chapter when dealing with discourse ethics, because discourse ethics is a post-conventional ethics.

There is not only an internal differentiation within the lifeworld, but also a differentiation between lifeworld and system (and the system is in turn increasingly internally differentiated into systems). The lifeworld is reproduced through communicative action and language. Although the internal differentiation of the lifeworld can deal with some of the increasing complexity of modern societies (for instance, in the form of abstract norms that are not tied to particular contexts), this increasing complexity leads to a differentiation – or 'uncoupling' – between lifeworld and system (ibid., 153ff.). The system 'relieves' the lifeworld mechanism of communicative action of some of the burden of integrating society (ibid., 181).

The system – or better: systems – is not integrated through the medium of language or through communicative action. Instead it is integrated through non-linguistic steering media, most importantly money and power. System action is not governed by an orientation towards mutual understanding, but by consequences, which can be intentional as well as non-intentional. The most important examples of systems are the market and the state, which are integrated through the steering media of money and power, respectively. The steering media are the media through which action is coordinated, and, in the case of systems, this is done through the consequences of actions, and this works in an impersonal fashion. For instance, my bank will not be interested in hearing my personal life history or about my need for a new garage. However, if they know that I can go elsewhere and get a (better) loan, they may give me a loan. Thus, the market regulates behaviour, and it does so in a way that happens, in a manner of speaking, behind the backs of the agents; that is, behaviour is coordinated through consequences of behaviour (for instance, lowering the interest rate on a loan). The coordination of agents' actions happens through everybody's instrumental pursuance of individual goals. Likewise, (state) power can be used to regulate people's behaviour, for instance through threats about punishment for financial misconduct or through bans on certain types of loans. Because systems work in this impersonal way, they can be much more efficient for the material reproduction of society than can lifeworld and communicative action, but the kind of rationality that systems can offer is instrumental and strategic rationality.

The concepts of lifeworld and system provide a dual perspective on society. Habermas does not reduce society to either lifeworld or systems. Unlike Niklas Luhmann, Habermas does not believe that society can be understood as made up simply of systems (Habermas 1987c, 368–85; 1996a, 48–52). However, there can be no modern, complex society without systems integration. The dual lifeworld and systems perspective can also be seen as a way to avoid the economism and reductionism of Marx's (1978) base-superstructure model, where the economic base determines what goes on in the legal, cultural and ideological superstructure. The conflicts and crises of contemporary societies cannot be understood as the outcome of class struggles in an economic base; rather, as we shall see in the next section, they are the outcome of tensions between lifeworld and systems.

Lifeworld and systems are at once substantive concepts and methodological perspectives. They are concepts that are meant to account for phenomena in modern societies. At the same time, they are also methodological perspectives because they describe the perspectives a researcher can take on society. The researcher can take a lifeworld perspective, where she takes a participant perspective as if she was a participant in the lifeworld of the agents she studies, trying to interpret and understand them. Or she can take a systems perspective, where she takes the objectivating perspective of an observer. The same phenomena can be studied from both perspectives, although any particular phenomena may lend itself more readily to study from one perspective rather than another. In this sense, the lifeworld-systems distinction is not just a distinction between real entities, but also an analytical distinction. Habermas's point is that, just as we need both lifeworld and systems to reproduce modern, complex societies, so we need both lifeworld and systems perspectives to get an adequate grip on contemporary society, including the pathologies of those societies.

THE PATHOLOGIES OF MODERNITY: THE COLONIZATION OF THE LIFEWORLD

Modernity leads to differentiation between and within the lifeworld and systems, and this in turn leads to rationalization. Importantly, what Habermas proposes is a differentiated conception of reason and rationalization, first of all because of the distinction between communicative and instrumental/strategic reason. Thus, when Weber, and Horkheimer and Adorno (2002) criticize rationalization in modern societies, Habermas can reply that their views of reason and modernity are one-sided because they only focus on one form of reason, namely instrumental/strategic reason.

Habermas is not uncritical of rationalization, however. But he is only critical of rationalization insofar as it is one-sided and has detrimental effects on communicative action and reason or, to be more precise, on the communicative reproduction of the lifeworld. Habermas precisely argues that communicative action and reason enjoy primacy over their instrumental and strategic siblings, and that the former contain an emancipatory promise.[8] Hence, he is critical of those cases where strategic action and reason substitute for their communicative counterparts. When this happens, it leads to a loss of communicative freedom, he argues, even if it may also lead to greater efficiency when it comes to the material reproduction of society.

In other words, the problem arises when systems organized around strategic action and reason encroach upon lifeworld structures that can only be reproduced communicatively. That is, when systemic imperatives drive out communicative action and reason from lifeworld domains that can only be reproduced and integrated communicatively. Paradoxically, '[t]he rationalization of the lifeworld makes possible the emergence and growth of subsystems whose independent imperatives turn back destructively upon the lifeworld itself' (Habermas 1987a, 186). Habermas refers to this encroachment of the systems on the lifeworld as the colonization of the lifeworld by systems or by systems imperatives. It happens when the communicative orientation towards mutual understanding is substituted by the instrumental and strategic orientation towards success (i.e. efficiency in achieving certain ends).

The colonization of the lifeworld can take different forms and have different effects, which are linked to the different functions of communicative action in the different structural components of the lifeworld (ibid., 141–3). Colonization can, first, lead to loss of meaning, that is, a breakdown in the cultural reproduction of the lifeworld. Second, it can lead to anomie, that is, breakdown of social norms and, hence, the social integration of society. And, finally, colonization can lead to psychopathologies in the context of the socialization of individuals and their personality.

Take as an example academia today, perhaps across the world, but certainly in Britain. Increasingly, the market logic is being rolled out across universities and education more generally. Universities must make money and the bottom line matters for their future. As a result, more and more things are measured in terms of time and outputs (such and such number of students per hour of teaching or per square metre of teaching space and so on). Teaching and research increasingly look like the commercial production of goods (education and research) to consumers (students and their parents, government and business). This also influences the relationship between students and professors. Whereas this relationship may have been communicative, it risks becoming increasingly strategic with agents asking questions such as: How can I make as much money on this student with the fewest possible resources? How can I maximize my chances of getting a decent degree with as little effort as possible? The relationship between student and professor is less and less one of transmitting knowledge and socializing the student into the world of knowledge and critical thinking and citizenship.

Another example – this time from Habermas – is welfare state provisions. These clearly often have an egalitarian thrust to them, and we can say that they have an emancipatory effect on those who enjoy them insofar as it makes them able to do things they would not otherwise have been able to do. For instance, if I fall ill, I am not necessarily forced out of work and forced to give up my house and live on skid row, because the state will provide health care, sick leave and so on. However, welfare state provisions also lead to legal regulation of lifeworld matters that were previously, and perhaps better, regulated through communicative action. The danger is that these provisions lead to what Habermas (ibid., 357) calls juridification (*Verrechtlichung*), which he defines as 'the tendency toward an increase in formal (or positive, written) law that can be observed in modern society'. 'From the start', he writes,

> [t]he *ambivalence of guaranteeing freedom and taking it away* has attached to the policies of the welfare state. . . . The negative effects of this . . . result *from the form of juridification itself.* It is now the very means of guaranteeing freedom that endangers the freedom of the beneficiaries. (ibid., 361f.)

It means that we become reduced to passive clients in our relations with the state. What we owe each other (in the family, civil society and in relation to the state) is reduced to rights that are not sensitive to the particularity of our particular situations.

What happens is this:

> The situation to be regulated is embedded in the context of a life history and of a concrete form of life; it has to be subjected to violent abstraction, not merely because it has to be subsumed under the law, but so that it can be dealt with administratively. (ibid., 363)

Although my particular case (of unemployment, medical problem and so on) has a complex set of meanings for me and for anyone taking a communicative ('lifeworld') perspective on it, for the state it is merely one more case to be subsumed under general rules, which the state does from on objectivating ('systems') perspective. The result is colonization of the lifeworld:

> The more the welfare state goes beyond pacifying the class conflict lodged in the sphere of production and spreads a net of client relationships over private spheres of life, the stronger are the anticipated pathological side effects of a juridification that entails both a bureaucratization and a monetarization of core areas of the lifeworld. (ibid., 364)

Habermas (ibid., 370) concludes that '[i]t is the medium of law itself that violates the communicative structures of the sphere that has been juridified'. Strictly speaking Habermas does not believe that *all* legal regulation ('the medium of law itself') leads to colonization. Rather what is meant is that there are things that cannot adequately be integrated through the medium of law (and power), or if they are, it will result in pathologies. That is, there are things within the lifeworld that are essentially communicative and can only be regulated and integrated through communicative action; medical treatment would be an example of this. It is not the medium of law as such that leads to colonization, but the misapplication or overly eager application of law to lifeworld contexts that leads to colonization. Later, in *Between Facts and Norms* (1996a), Habermas further qualifies his view of law when he argues that the law can have a communicative foundation insofar as it has been established through deliberations among those who are subject to it. This makes him able to distinguish between legitimate and illegitimate law, or in the terms of *The Theory of Communicative Action*, between non-colonizing and colonizing law.

Apart from juridification, the colonization of the lifeworld also consists in cultural impoverishment. As a result of the rationalization of the lifeworld, there is a differentiation of expert cultures in the areas of science and technology, morality and law, and art (Habermas 1984, 159ff.). These areas are differentiated from one another and from the rest of the lifeworld. While this enhances the self-reflexivity of society, it also results in the creation of elites that are removed from ordinary citizens, who in turn become removed from authoritative deliberations on matters of truth, rightness and aesthetic expression. (Think here of statements such as 'I'll leave that to those who know something about it . . .'.) The creation of expert cultures robs the public sphere and the everyday life of ordinary citizens of their critical potential. As in agents' relationships with the welfare state, the result here is passivity. In this way, cultural impoverishment undermines the critical public sphere, which as we saw in Chapter 2 is so important to Habermas (1989a), and which may otherwise have created a counterweight to the systems.

The colonization thesis has the advantage that it avoids the economic reductionism of orthodox Marxism. Habermas (1987a, 347–9) does not reduce the pathologies of contemporary capitalist society to an economic base or to class conflicts, although the colonization thesis is still linked to an analysis of capitalist society. Thus, revolution in the classical Marxist sense would not resolve the problems of colonization. It is impossible to turn back the clock on the differentiation between and within lifeworld and system; there cannot be a modern, complex society without differentiation and without systems. Habermas is not critical of differentiation and systems as such, only of cases where these developments are one-sided and where they lead to colonization of the lifeworld. The state and the market are here to stay, even if we would be better off with a democratized state and a social-democratically regulated market. In this too, Habermas (ibid., 338–43) distinguishes his position from that of Marx and many Marxists.

Colonization does not lead to class conflicts in the traditional Marxist sense, but to new lines of conflict over new issues. Those conflicts and issues are situated at the border between lifeworld and system, where the system encroaches upon the lifeworld. Here is how Habermas (ibid., 392) describes these conflicts and issues:

In the past decade or two [since 1981], conflicts have developed in advanced Western societies that deviate in various ways from the welfare-state pattern of institutionalized conflict over distribution. They no longer flare up in domains of material reproduction; they are no longer channeled through parties and associations; and they can no longer be allayed by compensations. Rather, these new conflicts arise in domains of cultural reproduction, social integration, and socialization . . . The issue is not primarily one of compensations that the welfare state can provide, but of defending and restoring endangered ways of life. In short, the new conflicts are not ignited by distribution problems but by questions having to do with the grammar of forms of life.[9]

These new lines of conflict do not pertain to redistribution of material goods, and the struggles are not for material compensation from the welfare state. Instead they arise in the context of the three structural components of the lifeworld and the functions that take place there: culture, society and personality, and cultural reproduction, social integration and socialization. In this way, the distinctions Habermas makes in his theory of communicative action and the lifeworld serve to identify and diagnose the problems of contemporary society. The problems point to new collective agents as well. Rather than classes and class-based parties, new social movements become important as channels for discontent with the colonization of the lifeworld (ibid., 393–6).[10]

Habermas's position is also different from that of conservatives. Habermas argues that we must distinguish the destruction of traditional forms of life from the destruction of post-conventional and post-traditional forms of life. Only the latter is problematic, and the disappearance of traditional forms of life should not be taken as a loss. The colonization thesis relates to the destruction of post-conventional lifeworlds that have achieved a certain level of rationalization. So, the difference between Habermas and the conservatives is that Habermas sees post-traditional, rationalized lifeworlds as the relevant alternative to the growth of systems, whereas the conservatives see both the growth of systems and the rationalization of the lifeworld as a loss (Habermas 1989b).

Before moving on to look at what Habermas thinks needs to be done, there are two critical points worth mentioning. There is first the criticism that Habermas is insufficiently critical of capitalism and the systems of the market and the (capitalist) state. Although Habermas is critical of colonization, he accepts the market and the state as such, and he takes them as unavoidable elements of a modern, complex society. Thereby, the critique goes, he reifies existing social structures, because he is only concerned with where to draw the line between system and lifeworld imperatives rather than getting rid of the system imperatives altogether. This makes his approach too defensive, even conservative, where he ought not to have given up on the revolutionary potential of Marxism (for instance, McCarthy 1985; Shabani 2003).

A related critique has been raised by theorists inspired by Michel Foucault (see Kelly 1994). Foucault was also concerned with the ways in which apparent progress and emancipation in fact hides new modes of subjection and unfreedom. Although he did not use the same terms as Habermas, Foucault was also concerned with the ways in which juridification guarantees freedom with one hand and takes it away with the other. There is an important difference between Foucault and Habermas however. Habermas distinguishes between the regulative force of law and the constitutive force of law. The former is linked to the use of law in already existing practices, where the legal regulations 'stand in a continuum with moral norms and are superimposed on communicatively structured areas of action. They give to these informally constituted domains of action a binding form backed by state sanction' (Habermas 1987a, 366). The constitutive force of law is linked to the way in which systems constitute new areas for legal regulation by subjecting them to the medium of law. The distinction is subtle, but important for Habermas. It is effectively a distinction between law that is embedded in communicative lifeworld contexts and law that is rooted in system imperatives. If Habermas can distinguish in this way between legal regulation that guarantees freedom and legal regulation that reduces freedom, then he has a way to argue that the problem is not law as such, but the imperatives it serves (communicative freedom or instrumental and strategic rationality).

Foucault, however, does not believe that it is possible to distinguish the two forms of legal regulation – and hence lifeworld and systems – so easily. For him, the regulative force of law is also constitutive. Whereas Habermas believes that it is possible to isolate an emancipatory form of legal regulation, for Foucault emancipation through law always goes hand in hand with subjection. For him, there is no such thing as a power-free discourse that can form the basis for law that does not also constitute the subjects and the relationships among subjects in the lifeworld, thus encroaching on the discursive formation of law from the outside. Whereas for the later Habermas of *Between Facts and Norms* (1996a) it is possible to root law in communicative power, for Foucault communicative power cannot be completely distinguished from strategic power.[11]

CONCLUSION: WHAT IS TO BE DONE?

The Theory of Communicative Action paints a fairly pessimistic picture of contemporary Western societies. It is far from as pessimistic as was Horkheimer and Adorno's (2002) *Dialectic of Enlightenment*, but at the same time it does not point beyond capitalism or the imperatives of money and power. In that sense, it is a defensive approach. Subsequent to *The Theory of Communicative Action*, Habermas (1996a, 486f) referred to a 'siege' model for the protection of the lifeworld from the systems, and he also talked of building 'restraining barriers' to protect the lifeworld against the encroachment of the systems (Habermas 1987c, 364). He thinks of the relationship between lifeworld and systems as one of a border conflict. The idea was to build a dam around the lifeworld in order to keep out the systems media and protect it from these. Rather than doing away with the systems, it is a matter of shifting the position of the border between lifeworld and systems while accepting the existence of the systems of the market and the state.

At the same time, Habermas suggested that law can be rooted in the communicative action in the lifeworld. He talked of 'building in sensors for the exchanges between lifeworld and system' (ibid.; see also 1992a, 444; 1996a, 484). What he has in mind are sensors that can channel communicatively generated will from the lifeworld into the systems, so that the latter will be guided by communicative power at least to some extent. It does not do away with the systems, but it is a less defensive strategy, and it is the strategy Habermas has subsequently followed (see Habermas 1997, 134–6). In *Between Facts and Norms*, Habermas argues more extensively that legal power can be rooted in what he now calls the communicative power of the lifeworld, especially a well-functioning public sphere and civil society. In this way, law is subsumed to the imperatives of communicative action and reason (namely mutual understanding), and it makes possible rational and autonomous law that can, at least in theory, integrate society without pathological side effects. This more offensive – and optimistic – approach recalls the importance of new social movements, which Habermas already highlighted in *The Theory of Communicative Action*, as well as the importance of the public sphere, which was the topic of Habermas's (1989a) first book on *The Structural Transformation of the Public Sphere*.

Is Habermas too pessimistic? Or too optimistic? The answer to those questions will depend on your diagnosis of the present and on the goals you believe a critical theory should work to realize. Habermas's work – for instance in *The Theory of Communicative Action* – itself relies on a particular diagnosis of contemporary society and a set of goals for critical theory (see Habermas 1987a, 374–403 on 'The Tasks of a Critical Theory of Society'). For instance, in one place he says about socialism, linking it to the conceptual apparatus of the theory of communicative action and lifeworld/system: 'that which for me constitutes the idea of socialism is the possibility of overcoming the propensity for one-sidedness of the rationalization process' (Habermas in Horster and van Reijen 1992, 99; see also Habermas 1991; 1997, 139–42). Habermas holds on to some notion of socialism and to an analysis of capitalism, but it is a revised Marxism that interprets emancipation and rationalization in a different way from that of Marx and orthodox Marxism.

FURTHER READINGS

Although *The Theory of Communicative Action* is long and offers much more detail than most students need, it is not as difficult to read as one might at first think. Particularly useful are the more systematic chapters (the 'Introduction', the two 'Intermediate Reflections' and the 'Concluding Reflections'). For Habermas's other writings on communicative action and reason, see his *On the Pragmatics of Communication* (1998a), chapters 1, 3–4 and 7 and *On the Pragmatics of Social Interaction* (2001a). The best introduction to *The Theory of Communicative Action* and to Habermas's work during this period is David Ingram's (1987) *Habermas and the Dialectic of Reason*. Also useful is Thomas McCarthy's 'Translator's Introduction' in the first volume of *The Theory of Communicative Action*. Stephen K. White's *The Recent work of Jürgen Habermas* (1989, chapters 1–2 and 5) introduces Habermas's theory of communicative action and reason in the context of discussions about modernity, and David Rasmussen's *Reading Habermas* (1990, chapters 1–3) usefully explains Habermas's project and method. The best collections of essays discussing *The Theory of Communicative Action* are Honneth and Joas (1991), *Communicative Action* and Honneth et al. (1992), *Philosophical Investigations in the Unfinished Project of Enlightenment.*

CHAPTER FOUR

DISCOURSE ETHICS

INTRODUCTION

In the early 1980s, and on the basis of the theory of communicative action and reason, Habermas developed his theory of discourse ethics. As the name suggests, it is an ethics, that is, a theory of how to address practical questions of how one ought to act. It is also *discourse* ethics in that the answers to practical questions are to be found through discourse where only the forceless force of the better argument reigns.

Habermas's discourse ethics relates to themes addressed in the previous chapters. First, his discourse ethics can be said to be a part of a Critical Theory of society in that it provides a way of approaching practical questions, and that it involves a reflexive attitude and a yardstick of critique, namely rational discourse and consensus. As we shall see, Habermas draws increasingly on Kant's philosophy; that said, he also draws on insights from Hegel and insists that ethics must be intersubjective. Furthermore, and in contrast to Horkheimer and Adorno's later work, Habermas's discourse ethics provides a positive ethics, although it is not meant to be substantial, but only procedural, providing a procedure for generating rational answers to practical questions.

Second, the discourse ethics is linked to the ideal of the public sphere. Discourse ethics expresses the idea of the force of the public use of reason in the area of ethics. Habermas makes the point that the public, or discursive, use of reason has a peculiar force when it comes to practical questions: it can generate rational answers to those questions. Seen in this way, discourse ethics is one way to explicate the idea and the idealizations of the public sphere, since it makes explicit the idea that emancipation and reason are internally linked to inclusion and equality.

Third, the theory of communicative action and reason provides the basis for Habermas to develop his ideas in other areas. In this case, discourse ethics extends the theory of communicative action and reason to practical questions, especially morality. Much of the groundwork for this is already present in the theory of communicative action and reason: the formal pragmatics, the notions of communicative action and reason, and discourse. Finally, Habermas's discourse ethics is the link between the theory of communicative action and reason and his discourse theory of law and democracy, which he was to develop from the late 1980s onwards. That is the subject of the following chapter.

The present chapter is structured as follows. I first explain some basic philosophical terms that are important for the way Habermas approaches the whole issue of ethics. Next I explain how Habermas moves from communicative action via communicative rationality to rational discourse and rational consensus. Here I explain the main concepts of discourse ethics, including the discourse principle and the universalization principle. Having done so, I explain an important distinction that Habermas makes within discourse ethics between pragmatic, ethical and moral questions. The subsequent section considers three of Habermas's sources of inspiration for his discourse ethics: Durkheim, Mead and Kohlberg. With the help of these, Habermas tries to link his argument for discourse ethics to an account of the development of individuals and societies. Finally, the last four sections of the chapter examine four different criticisms that have been made of Habermas's discourse ethics.

FOUR REQUIREMENTS FOR A DISCOURSE THEORY OF MORALITY

Before laying out the basic concepts of Habermas's discourse ethics, it is useful to examine some of the requirements that Habermas sets himself for his ethics and, in the process, to clarify some key philosophical terms. Habermas (1990, 120–2, 196–8) believes that an ethics must be deontological, cognitivist, formal and universal, and he believes that his discourse ethics can meet each of these challenges.

It is customary to distinguish between deontology and teleology. As the term suggests, teleology is concerned with a telos, that is, a goal.

In ethical terms, teleology is concerned with the good, and justice is relative to a given good, whether the benefit of society (for utilitarians) or the maintenance of a tradition (for communitarians). The term deontology is from the Greek 'deon', meaning duty or obligation. This is precisely what a deontological ethics is: an ethics of duty or obligation. That is, it is an ethics of the right, of what it is right to do irrespective of any good or telos. A deontological ethics stipulates what we ought to do – that is, what we are obliged to do – irrespective of our particular goals or interests. The most important example of a deontological ethics is Kant's moral philosophy. Habermas, then, believes that an ethics must be deontological in this sense that justice (the right) is independent of, and has priority over, the good; the right trumps the good. Discourse ethics, for instance, is not dependent on a particular way of life and the conceptions of the good inherent to that way of life, he argues.

An ethics must also be cognitivist, Habermas argues. This means that questions of practical nature – What should I/we do? How should we act? – can be treated in such a way that we can treat the answers we come up with as rational answers: 'normative rightness must be regarded as a claim to validity that is analogous to a truth claim' (ibid., 197). For Habermas, just as we can talk about this or that validity claim as true (or untrue), so we can talk of normative validity claims as right (or wrong) in an analogous manner. It is important to emphasize that Habermas does not think that truth and normative rightness are the same; it is precisely an analogy. The objects of the two kinds of validity claims are not constituted in the same way. What is right is right because it has been established as such through discourse; this is so in a way that is not the case with claims to truth about the world. However, both kinds of validity can be treated as a matter of discursive vindication of validity claims. In this way, Habermas (ibid., 120) believes, it is possible to talk about rationality and 'knowledge' (hence 'cognitivism') in relation to ethics: 'moral-practical issues can be decided on the basis of reasons'.

Given the pluralism of moral views that exist in today's societies, Habermas believes that an ethics for modern societies cannot give substantive answers to moral questions. That is, an ethics cannot be a set of substantive norms telling us how to act. In this sense, an ethics should be formalist. For Habermas, this means that it should provide a procedure for deciding moral questions, and this is why Habermas reconstructs a *procedure* of argumentation by asking what the structures of argumentation are that will yield rational and legitimate answers to moral questions. His discourse ethics is, then, not meant to say what the answers should be, only how we should find them. In this sense, it is a procedural and minimal ethics.

Finally, an ethics should be universalist. It should not be tied to a particular community or era, but should be universal across space and time, at least in its intention. In a word, it should not be ethnocentric: 'I must prove that my moral principle is not just a reflection of the prejudices of adult, white, well-educated, Western males of today' (ibid., 197). In this way, Habermas hopes to avoid the imperialistic and violent imposition of norms on individuals and minority groups.

FROM COMMUNICATIVE ACTION TO RATIONAL DISCOURSE AND CONSENSUS

To understand Habermas's argument for discourse ethics, it is necessary to go back to the argument for communicative action and reason. Recall that Habermas argues that it is impossible to envisage something like society without communicative action. Without communicative action as a way to coordinate action, society would fall apart and social interaction would break down. In the long run, no society can exist on the basis of strategic action – including lies, deception and violence – alone. So, there is no alternative to communicative action in the long run if we want something like a stable and peaceful society, or if we want to explain how this is possible.

Now, recall also the quote from the 'Appendix' to *Knowledge and Human Interests*, where Habermas (1987b, 314; see also above p. 29) states that as social, and thereby communicating, beings, something like rational discourse and consensus are posited for, and by, us. With respect to the unavoidability of communicative action and its presuppositions, Habermas (2001b, 13f.) states:

> The necessity of this 'must' has a Wittgensteinian rather than a Kantian sense. That is, it does not have the transcendental sense of universal, necessary, and noumenal [*intelligiblen*] conditions of possible experience, but has the grammatical sense of an 'inevitability' stemming from the conceptual connections of a system of learned – but for us inescapable [*nicht hintergehbar*] – rule-governed behavior. After the pragmatic deflation of the Kantian

approach, 'transcendental analysis' means the search for presumably universal, but only de facto inescapable conditions that must
be met for certain fundamental practices or achievements. All
practices for which we cannot imagine functional equivalents in
our sociocultural forms of life are 'fundamental' in this sense.

The point Habermas is making is that communicative action (and
the assumptions about rationality and discourse that comes with it)
is not just one practice among others, because it has a special status.
We cannot avoid communicative action in the long run if we want
peaceful social interaction, which is in turn necessary for having
something like a society. Habermas (2001a, 147) also talks about the
'lack of alternatives' to communicative action and discourse.

The argument that takes us from communicative action to discourse goes like this. Within the implicit consensus of the lifeworld,
disagreement may arise whereby a specific aspect of the lifeworld is
problematized (for instance, whether one ought to switch off one's
mobile during a lecture). When things are thematized or problematized in this way, we move to discourse where the validity of a norm
is no longer taken for granted. In discourse, participants argue for
and against validity claims under more or less idealized conditions.
The validity claims have a Janus-faced character to them: on the one
hand, they are raised in particular contexts and informed by particular interests; on the other hand, they point beyond any particular
context towards a potentially universal communication community
who will test whether we are dealing with a universalizable interest:
'in ever wider forums before an ever more competent and larger audience against ever new objections' (Habermas 2001c, 36).

If the discourse meets certain conditions, then we have what
Habermas calls a rational discourse. The conditions are that everybody potentially affected is included on an equal footing, that they
all have a voice and can make any objection they want, and that they
be sincere about their voiced opinions.[1] When it comes to rational
discourse, there can be neither internal nor external constraints on
the discourse: 'only the unforced force of the better argument' counts
(Habermas 1993, 163). The outcome of a rational discourse may be
a rational consensus, which all participants in the discourse have
agreed to under the conditions that regulate rational discourse (full
information, equality and so on).

Recall Habermas's performative contradiction argument. He uses this in the context of discourse ethics to argue that when you enter into discourse, or argumentation, you have already made certain assumptions and have in effect already signed up to certain norms that characterize discourse. In this way, you cannot argue against those same norms, and the point of the performative contradiction argument is to show that the presuppositions of discourse are unavoidable or inescapable. Relying on an argument by Karl-Otto Apel, Habermas refers to this argument for discourse ethics as a 'transcendental-pragmatic' argument. It is transcendental only in a weak sense, and it takes discourse as a practice and starts from this practice and asks what one must assume when entering into this practice, that is, when practicing discourse (Habermas 1990, 79–82).

With this, Habermas believes that he has shown a necessary link between communicative action, validity claims, discourse, rational discourse and rational consensus. Indeed, the promise of a rational consensus is inherent, if also implicit, to communication from the word go. This was already hinted at in the 'Appendix' to *Knowledge and Human Interests* (1987b, 314), as we have seen. The promise of a rational consensus where the forceless force of the better argument has ruled also means that the practice of discourse may be said to be rational and even emancipatory. We may be engaged in local practices of discourse here and now, but these discourses are characterized by conditions or structures that are characteristic of all such discourses and constitute the discourses as such. Thus, what we are doing cannot be reduced to local customs or exercise of power.

What is more, Habermas believes that he has solved a problem in Kant. In *Knowledge and Human Interests*, Habermas (ibid., 380) links the idea of the rational consensus to Kant's 'fact of reason':

[I]t is evidently a fact of nature that the human species, confined to its sociocultural form of life, can only reproduce itself through the medium of that most unnatural idea, truth, which necessarily begins with the counterfactual assumption that universal agreement is *possible*. Since empirical speech is only *possible* by virtue of the fundamental norms of rational speech, the cleavage between a real and an inevitably idealized (if only hypothetically ideal) community of language is built not only into the process of argumentative reasoning but into the very life-praxis of social systems.

In this way, perhaps the Kantian notion of the fact of reason can be revitalized.

With the concepts of communicative action and discourse, Habermas believes that he has overcome the Kantian opposition between real and ideal, because this opposition moves inside social practice, so to speak. The ideal is 'actually efficacious' as a presupposition we make when engaging in actual communicative action and discourse; the ideal is then not something foreign to the particular practice (Habermas 2001c, 35, emphasis removed). In this way, the ideal – the interest in reason – need not be posited as a transcendental Idea in Kant's sense, involving the distinction between the noumenal and the phenomenal. Instead the ideal is always already at work in what makes us human beings, namely our use of language. Rational consensus, then, works both as a regulative idea (in the sense of a fact of reason that gives a telos to communication) and as a critical ideal. As a critical ideal, it is only a counterfactual ideal that is 'actually effective in ways that point beyond the limits of actual situations' (ibid., 13, emphasis removed). In Habermas's terms, the idea/ideal is detranscendentalized or immanentized.

Rational consensus, then, is constitutive of communicative action (and indirectly of language as such), but only in a weak sense of counterfactual 'idealizing suppositions we cannot avoid making' (ibid., emphasis removed). The idea of rational consensus makes us able to distinguish right from wrong, just from unjust, and to do so in a way that we can call rational. In this way, the idea of rational consensus functions as a critical ideal. It also makes us able to see discourse as a learning process where ever more competent participants come up with answers that are, therefore, ever more rational. The ideas of rational discourse and rational consensus provides us a way to distinguish between norms that are right (because equally good for all) and norms that are relative to a particular way of life. It does so because the rational discourse must be a universal, or at least an ever-widening, discourse, and so it always puts a question mark above any particular consensus that we may have reached (is it really just a consensus among 'us', among White European intellectuals? And so on). In this way, norms can be treated as more than just facts or as just valid 'for us'. We can treat them in a cognitivist sense because we can discuss their validity and rationality, and we can do so in such a way that we can say that the end-result is more rational than what we started with. In this sense, we can distinguish the validity from the mere acceptance of norms.

We now come to the two key principles of discourse ethics: the discourse principle (D) and the universalization principle (U). These form part of the language theoretical argument for discourse ethics, and help make sense of discourse ethics.

The discourse principle (D) tells us how the validity of norms is to be achieved, namely through practical discourse. It reads: 'Only those norms can claim to be valid that meet (or could meet) with the approval of all affected in their capacity *as participants in a practical discourse*' (Habermas 1990, 66; see also 93, 120; 1996a, 107). In this way, the discourse principle both concerns the common good and individual dignity: we can arrive at a notion of the common good, but every individual must give their consent and must do so severally.

The universalization principle (U) tells us how to test the universalizability of moral norms. As such it should be distinguished from the democratic principle, which tells us how to test legal norms; this is the subject of the next chapter on deliberative democracy. The universalization principle reads: 'For a norm to be valid, the consequences and side effects that its *general* observance can be expected to have for the satisfaction of the particular interests of *each* person affected must be such that *all* affected can accept them freely' (Habermas 1990, 120; compare the slightly different formulation at p. 65). The norm must be universal ('all'), but the flipside of this is that it must be acceptable to 'each' person taken individually.

Notice that universality does not consist in the correspondence between the moral norm and some transcendental realm; the universalization test is not meant to discover some already existing universal norm, but to generate universal norms. The universalization principle is formal in that it gives us a procedure stipulating the conditions that, if met, will yield universal answers to moral questions. The universalization principle does not itself give us particular norms. Notice also that the principle has a dialogical aspect to it. The testing of moral norms is not monological, as in Kant, where an individual imagines if he could will the maxim of his action to be a universal law and thereby establishes what is equally good for all.

Finally, the universalization test does not avoid the particular interests 'of *each* person', as it says. This is again in opposition to Kant who did not want to introduce interests into the equation because he wanted to avoid teleology and empiricism of any kind.

At most, Kant would speak of an 'interest' in reason. Habermas (1987b, 380) too speaks of an interest in reason: the fact of reason is posited to us as communicating beings. However, Habermas believes that it is also possible to discuss particular interests in discourse. Importantly, those interests are not simply given, but can be discussed and, thereby, changed (through discourse, I may come to think differently about mobiles in public spaces such as a lecture hall, for instance). In discourse, the participants' particular interests are not bracketed behind a veil of ignorance as in John Rawls's (1971) theory of justice. For Habermas, discourse, as expressed in the universalization principle, is precisely about the universalizability of particular interests. We can think of those interests in terms of validity claims, and what the universalization test does is to test whether those interests or validity claims can be universalized or not. That is, the test is whether certain given interests are not simply my or our interests, but the equal interests of all – in short, whether they are universal.

According to Habermas, the incorporation of interests into discourse solves a problem of motivation that Kant faces: why be moral? The problem arises if we cannot have a particular, personal interest in morality because morality has been divided from interest. In Habermas's discourse ethics, interests are not left at the door, so to speak. The universal moral norms that we arrive at are linked to particular interests. They have emerged from a discussion of those particular interests, and they will also be 'my' or 'our' interests and not just the interests of an abstract and impersonal 'all'.

Together, these different elements of discourse ethics – rational discourse and consensus, the discourse and universalization principles – make clear how discourse ethics is, first, rooted in a theory of action and language, and, second, cognitivist, formal and universalist.

To round off this initial characterization of discourse ethics, consider the case of animals (Habermas 1993, 106–11; 2003b, 33). With its emphasis on the public use of reason and on autonomy as rational self-legislation, it would seem that discourse ethics has no place for animals. Nevertheless, Habermas believes that it is possible to articulate a discourse ethical approach to animals and nature. The central question is whether we can think of animals as moral beings on a par with human beings. Habermas locates morality in an intersubjectivist account of human life, and so the question is if animals can enter into the same kind of intersubjective, moral relations that human beings are capable of.

Habermas's answer is a qualified one. It is possible to relate morally to animals, but the relationship is necessarily an asymmetrical one and so it must be distinguished from the moral relationship that human beings can have with one another. The reason is that we can speak of bodily integrity in relation to animals, but not personal integrity (Habermas 1993, 109). That is, morality and personal integrity is something more than bodily integrity. Animals enter into our (moral) world, but our relationship with them cannot be one of participants in a dialogue. Here it is worth quoting Habermas (ibid., 109f.) at length:

> There exists a quasi-moral responsibility toward animals that we encounter in the role (if not *completely* filled) of a second person, whom we look upon as if it were an alter ego. We can adopt a performative attitude toward many animals, though not toward plants. In that case, they are no longer objects to be observed by us, or even just objects of our empathy, but beings who, in their interaction with us, make their distinctive mode of being felt in a manner different than a rock does its mineral hardness or a plant does the osmotic interaction of an organism with its environment. To the extent that animals participate in our interactions, we enter into a form of contact that goes beyond one-sided or reciprocal observation because it is *of the same kind* as an intersubjective relation.

The moral status of animals in discourse ethics is one between humans and inanimate nature. Yet, even if animals can arouse moral feelings in us, they can never be equal participants in a moral dialogue, not even in theory. And this is after all where Habermas locates morality and reason: in the public use of reason. At most, animals can have a moral status that is *analogous* to that of human beings.

PRAGMATIC, ETHICAL AND MORAL QUESTIONS

Discourse ethics is not only about morality and moral norms, but has a wider application. This corresponds to a differentiation between different dimensions of practical discourse or different questions that can be raised vis-à-vis an issue in practical discourse: pragmatic, ethical and moral (Habermas 1993, 8–14; 1996a, 159–68).[2]

Here one must first distinguish practical discourse from theoretical discourse. Whereas theoretical discourse is about the objective world and truth, practical discourse is about what I or we should do, that is, how we should act, and its results are only truth-analogous. It is within practical discourse – and, so, within discourse ethics – that Habermas distinguishes between three kinds of questions that can be raised, namely pragmatic, ethical and moral questions.

In the case of pragmatic questions, we start from given goals and preferences and then ask what the most efficient means of meeting them are. Here it is a matter of purposive rationality, that is, instrumental and strategic reason. Take for instance the example of the professor and the student from the last chapter. The professor may challenge the student's assertion that he will hand in his essay the following day; for instance, he may point out that the university will be closed. The discourse may continue with the professor telling the student that she will be in, but that the student needs to call first in order for the professor to be able to open the door to the building for the student. This is an example of discourse participants taking a pragmatic perspective; goals and preferences are not in question when taking the pragmatic perspective, only the means of realizing them are.

The ethical and moral dimensions of discourse are more important and have been subject to more attention by Habermas (1990, 195ff.; 1993, chapter 1; 1996a, 159–64) himself and commentators on his work. The ethical concerns what is good for me or us in the long run and in relation to a tradition or a way of life. This is why Habermas talks about ethical-existential questioning, where it is a matter of ethical self-expression, that is, of finding out how I or we should live. Ethical questioning is about self-understanding – Who am I? Who are we? – although it takes place not just in intra-group discussions, but also in exchanges with other groups. Taking an ethical perspective, we cannot come up with universal answers because the ethical perspective is always linked to a particular individual or collective subject, and there is a plurality of these subjects in the world. To claim universality for the results of ethical questioning would result in the imperialistic imposition of values on others. The ethical is about values, that is, about good or bad, and the values are always relative to other values and to a way of life. Importantly, values are not simply given once and for all. We start the ethical questioning from certain values that are important for us, but the point of the ethical-existential discourse is to clarify these values, and this is not simply a matter of discovering who we are, but also of (re)creating the values and, thereby, a sense of who we are.

As opposed to the ethical, the moral concerns what is equally good for all, that is, what is right or just. The moral perspective is not relative to any particular subject, but is purely intersubjective. Moral reasons are supposedly equally good for all, and are not reasons that are only good for me or for us. The moral perspective is concerned with moral self-legislation, and norms can be right or wrong (as opposed to good or bad) and they have an absolute or unconditional character. The moral perspective involves an egalitarian and potentially universal discourse, which can at least in theory lead to a rational consensus where everybody has given his or her agreement to the outcome (think here of the universalization principle). Crucially, the moral perspective is not neutral, but has normative implications because it is internally connected to the concept of autonomy understood as rational self-legislation. The moral perspective is mediated by rational discourse as described above, and in this way it is not just one ethical value or perspective among others, but is supposed to be neutral vis-à-vis ethical values. In this sense, the moral perspective is deontological, whereas the ethical perspective has a teleological character.

The example of the professor and the student may help shed light on the distinction between ethical and moral aspects or perspectives. The example throws up ethical questions such as what sort of institution the particular university is. For instance, at stake may be whether the university in question is, or should be, one that values a law and order attitude where one should follow rules with no exceptions and so not allow late submission of essays. However, we can also imagine the professor and the student debating whether it is fair (i.e. just or right) that some students can hand in their essays later than others, or whether fairness requires that we take into consideration the particular circumstances of each student. Here the perspective is moral insofar as we ask what is equally good for all.

Another example – torture – also throws up both ethical and moral issues. A people or state may ask what sort of people or state it is to allow torture, or it may ask how to value life and pain and violence. These considerations may in turn have arisen from pragmatic considerations where it was a matter of finding the most effective way to realize specific goals (say, to avoid a perceived terrorist threat).

The ethical considerations may lead the citizens to take a moral perspective and ask what is equally good for all. Here one would not be able to exclude a priori the perspective of the potentially tortured persons because the moral perspective is at least potentially universal and so every person is potentially one of 'us' understood as an ever-widening communication community. This is what distinguishes the moral perspective: we must be able to put ourselves in the place of each and every other individual. Or, if we are debating the morality of torture, we must view ourselves as someone potentially at the receiving end of torture.

According to Habermas, the moral perspective has priority over the ethical perspective. The moral trumps the ethical if there is a clash between the two as in the example of torture. This is so because we may come to an understanding of who we are and what we value, but there is then an additional question we must address given that we live in a pluralist world. Given the pluralism of values and ethical perspectives, and given that we must coordinate action despite this pluralism, we must then also take the moral perspective. Here the moral perspective trumps the ethical perspective because the ethical one cannot deliver answers that are equally good for all irrespective of their particular values and conceptions of the good life. So it is not enough to argue that this is the way we do things around here; we need the moral perspective in order to coordinate action with other ways of life.

With this tripartite division of discourse ethics between pragmatic, ethical and moral perspectives, it should also be clear that the term 'discourse ethics' is actually a bit of a misnomer (Habermas 1990, vii). Discourse ethics is concerned with all three aspects of practical questions: the pragmatic, the ethical and the moral. As such, it is not merely concerned with the ethical as the term might suggest; nor is it simply concerned with the moral, deontological perspective even though it is sometimes implicitly used in this way.

DEVELOPMENTAL LOGICS

Habermas supports his discourse ethics with a theory of language and it is also based on a theory of communicative action and reason. Among the sources Habermas draws on here is the work of his long-time collaborator and friend Karl-Otto Apel. Habermas seeks to support this language theoretical argument for discourse ethics with an account of the development of individuals and societies. Here he draws on Durkheim, Mead and Kohlberg among others. I shall not give an account of these theories here, but merely highlight some of the insights that Habermas takes from these theorists in order to bolster his language theoretical argument for discourse ethics.

Émile Durkheim

From the French sociologist Émile Durkheim (1858–1917), Habermas (1987a, 77–92) takes the idea of what he calls the linguistification of the sacred. This is part of Habermas's theory of modernity and, indirectly, of his theory of communicative action and reason on which discourse ethics is based. Habermas develops an account of the development of societies and especially of modernization; here his perspective is phylogenetic as he looks at the social evolution of the human species.

Durkheim's social theory spans a number of topics. What is important here is Durkheim's argument about the moral bindingness of norms. In pre-modern society, Durkheim argues, religion is the glue that holds society together. Norms are followed because they are taken to be sacred. People followed norms because they were sacred, not because they were backed by force; indeed, norms are backed by force because of their sacredness (ibid., 48ff.).

For Durkheim, modernity presents a problem because what happens when the sacred character of moral norms is gradually eroded with modernization? From where will norms get their binding character, if not from religion? Habermas's answer – which builds on Durkheim's own answer – is what he refers to as the linguistification of the sacred. Traditional norms may lose their binding character, but this need not lead to the dissolution of society, and one should certainly not hawk back to a lost, pre-modern lifeworld where norms are not problematized. The sacred character of norms is substituted by communicative reason. Norms are binding – because valid and rational – because they have been mediated by communicative reason, whether implicitly in the reproduction of the lifeworld through communicative action or explicitly through discursive problematization. This is why Habermas talks of linguistification: language and communication becomes the medium of social integration (together with systems, as we saw in the previous chapter). Not only does communicative action and reason substitute religion as the glue of society, but this can also be seen as progress – hence social evolution – because it involves a rationalization of the lifeworld. We should not, according to Habermas, think of this as a loss of the good old days.

The linguistification of the sacred is only a small part of Habermas's theory of modernity, but it shows the thrust of his argument: societies evolve, modernity involves rationalization of the lifeworld and of norms, and this in turn involves discourse, that is, the discursive testing of norms. In this way, discourse ethics is associated with rationalization and progress; it represents a step in the right direction in terms of social evolution.

George Herbert Mead

George Herbert Mead (1863–1931) was an American social psychologist who was also part of the philosophical current referred to as American pragmatism around the end of the nineteenth and the beginning of the twentieth centuries.[3] Mead asks how we human beings are able to use language, and not surprisingly this is a question that Habermas (ibid., chapter 5; 1992b, chapter 7) is also interested in.

Mead believes that language is more than just gestures and instinctive behaviour; we should look at language as meaningful action. For language to be successful, it assumes that the sender (the speaker) and the receiver (the hearer) understand the same from the same significant symbol, for instance the speech act 'I promise to . . .'. This requires that the speaker and the hearer are able to take the perspective of the other, that they are able to put themselves in the other's shoes. If we are able to take the perspective of the other, we are able to understand what the other means with the speech act. Of course this process of communication may break down, but then they switch to a process of clarification.

Taking the perspective of the other also accounts for the functioning of social norms. Here too one must be able to put oneself in others' shoes. Specifically, one must be able to take on different roles, what Mead refers to as ideal role taking. So, in the example of the professor and the student, the two of them must be able to take the perspective of the other and to put themselves in the role of a student and professor respectively. I must be able to master both my own role and the roles of others; that is, I must be able to master the expectations others have of me as well as the expectations linked to others' roles. This is what it takes to be able to master the norms that govern a particular area, and Mead refers to it as 'the generalized other'. When one is able to take the perspective of the generalized other, the norms have been internalized and also reconciled with one's own expectations. In this way, the norms become binding.

When looking at personality structures, Mead distinguishes between the 'me' and the 'I'. The 'me' refers to the social aspect of the personality, that is, to the fact that we are socialized beings. The 'I' refers to individuality, and it is especially visible in modern societies. Mead uses these terms to make sense of the way that social norms and expectations (the 'me') can be reconciled with individualism (the 'I). This reconciliation is possible, he argues, insofar as norms become more abstract and universal, and insofar as norms must pass through the deliberations of individuals taken as individuals. In this way, individuals become able to define roles and norms rather than being forced into pre-determined roles or being passively subject to norms.

Against the background of the account of discourse ethics above, it should be easy to see what Habermas finds appealing in Mead. The notion of ideal role taking helps Habermas explain the inter-subjective functioning of communication, and it helps him explain how rational discourse and the universalization test function. The account of modern personality structures helps Habermas show how discourse ethics need not emphasize either the social or the individual perspective at the expense of the other. And both ideas provide Habermas with the beginnings of an account of what is so special about modern personalities and societies that discourse ethics may be linked to actual developments in personality structures and societies.

Lawrence Kohlberg

The American psychologist Lawrence Kohlberg (1927–87) was interested in the development that a person goes through from being a child to being an adult. He thought of this development as a process of ever higher levels of consciousness, and he believed that this process was universal.

Kohlberg (1981, 409ff.; see also Habermas 1990, 123ff.) divides the child's development into three levels of moral development, and these three levels are in turn divided into two stages each. The three levels are pre-conventional, conventional and post-conventional.

The levels are differentiated according to two things: differentiation and integration. Differentiation refers to the child's ability to distinguish moral expectations from other expectations, for instance to differentiate morality from ethical life (equally good vs. how we do things around here). Integration refers to the ability to resolve moral conflicts by integrating conflicting claims, that is, by seeing an issue from the perspective of others. It is therefore linked by Habermas to Mead's notion of ideal role taking.

The point Kohlberg makes, and that Habermas takes on in the context of his discourse ethics, is that we can think of this development towards the post-conventional level of moral consciousness as the development of a conception of justice. We move from a conception of justice based on command and obedience through a conception of justice based on conformity to roles and norms to a conception of justice, at the post-conventional level, based on principles of justice (stage 5) and procedures for justifying norms (stage 6). Needless to say, Habermas believes that his discourse ethics belongs at stage 6, at the highest – most abstract and universal – level of moral development. Thus, Habermas's (1990, 33–41, 119–32, 172–88; 1993, chapter 3) appropriation of Kohlberg – together with his appropriation of Durkheim and Mead – helps him argue that discourse ethics is the most advanced theory of ethics available.

CRITIQUE I: THE PARADOX OF CONSENSUS

What follows in this and the following three sections are just some of the many criticisms that have been directed at Habermas's discourse ethics. The critiques are directed at discourse ethics, but to some degree they also apply to his theories of communicative action and reason and of deliberative democracy.

The first criticism concerns the status of the idea of rational consensus. Discourse ethics involves a number of idealizations, especially as regards rational discourse and rational consensus. However, the status of those idealizations has changed as Habermas has developed his theory. When he first proposed the formal pragmatic theory of language, Habermas sometimes held that rational discourse and consensus could be realized if only the circumstances were right. At other times, and in response to critics, he held that the idealizations may not be realisable in fact, but in theory they were, or that they could at least be approximated.[4] Following this view, the participants in discourse 'suppose that a rationally motivated agreement [that is, a rational consensus] could in principle be achieved, whereby the phrase "in principle" expresses the idealizing proviso: if only the argumentation could be conducted openly enough and continued long enough' (Habermas 1984, 42). Sometimes Habermas (1987c, 325, emphasis removed) would also refer to the idealizations as 'actually working fictions', which we presuppose, but which are impossible to realize: 'at once claimed and denied'. We must presuppose them and act as if they were realisable in order for the practice of discourse to work, but in fact they are utopian and will not be realized (1998a, 22f.; 1996a, 322f.). This view of the idealizations as counterfactual ideals can be found in Habermas's earlier work as well as in his more recent work.

In his most recent work, Habermas has gone one step further with respect to the ideal of rational consensus. Now he (sometimes) writes that a rational consensus is both empirically and conceptually impossible. He puts it in the following way: 'This entropic state of a definitive consensus, which would make all further communication superfluous, cannot be represented as a meaningful goal because it would engender paradoxes (an ultimate language, a final interpretation, a nonrevisable knowledge, etc.)' (Habermas 1996, 1518). A rational consensus is paradoxical because it would be the end to discourse, the end *of* discourse would be the end *to* discourse. Habermas (1998a, 365, quoting Wellmer 1998, 141) continues:

> Even if the ideal reference points are understood as aims that are not attainable in principle, or attainable only approximately, it remains 'paradoxical that we would be obliged to strive for the realization of an ideal whose realization would be the end of human history'.

That is, a rational – final – consensus actually contradicts the whole enterprise of discourse ethics; it would be the end to the very communication on the basis of which Habermas has developed his discourse ethics. In fact, one might argue that there is a kind of performative contradiction to the idea of rational consensus. The paradox is this: what makes communication possible (namely the implicit telos of a rational consensus) also makes it impossible and superfluous. If we had a rational consensus, there would be neither need nor room for further communication.

However, if that is the case, then it would seem that rational consensus cannot serve as the (only) goal of communication and discourse. Indeed, we can say that dissent or disagreement is equally important, because without it the source of communication would dry out, which is precisely why a rational consensus would be the end to communication. So, even if we believe that rational consensus is an essential part of communication and of discourse ethics, it cannot be the only goal of communication and discourse, and it cannot necessarily be prioritized over dissent.

This critique of Habermas – which Habermas has to some extent taken on board – is characteristic of Habermas's post-structuralist critics. They are sceptical about the idea of consensus in general because they are afraid that a consensus will be imposed on singularity and otherness. That is, they are afraid that a consensus is imposed on individuals and constituencies that are not part of the mainstream of society. At best, they argue, Habermas is inattentive to difference and dissent, at worst the effect of his discourse ethics is to impose consensus where there is none. This is a critique that has most famously and forcefully been put forward by the French philosopher Jean-François Lyotard (1984). In addition, some of these post-structuralist critics argue that the idea of a final consensus is self-contradictory in the way I have just presented it. For instance, Chantal Mouffe (2000, 48f.) has put forward this critique of Habermas's discourse ethics and deliberative democracy. Her conclusion is that it is not such a bad thing that a rational consensus is impossible, because what gives life to ethics and democracy is dissent and difference (see also Thomassen 2007, 27–33).

CRITIQUE II: JUSTIFICATION AND APPLICATION

Two criticisms often levelled at Kantian moral theories – including Habermas's – is that the moral law or perspective is too abstract to be meaningfully applied to social contexts, and that moral deliberation is too taxing because it requires that participants in moral discourse know everything about the circumstances and consequences of a given outcome (i.e. that discourse ethics asks too much of the participants in discourse). These criticisms reflect G.W.F. Hegel's (1977; see also Habermas 1990, 195–215; Finlayson 1999) critique of Kant. Hegel believed that morality must be concrete and must be embedded in ethical life (*Sittlichkeit*), and that social agents must be socialized into a moral way of life. As Hegel said, one cannot learn to swim before stepping into the water.[5]

In this section, I shall present one particular variation of this critique. It is a proposal by the German legal theorist Klaus Günther (1993), a proposal which Habermas (1993, 13f., 35–9; 1996a, 217–19) has subsequently taken up to modify his discourse ethics.

Günther proposes that we distinguish between two kinds of discourses: justification and application. In discourses of justification, we ask 'is it just?', that is, is it equally good for all? In discourses of application, we ask 'is it appropriate?' The two kinds of discourses are ordered sequentially. We first have the justification discourse where the focus is on the general justifiability of the norm, irrespective of particular cases. We then have the application discourse. It is necessary to add this second kind of discourse, because if the norm is not applied to concrete cases, then it would have no effect and could not guide action. In application discourse, the focus is on appropriateness, that is, on whether the norm is appropriate given the particular circumstances in which it is being applied. This is how Günther (quoted in Habermas 1993, 37) explains it:

> In justification only the norm itself, independently of its application in a particular situation, is relevant. The issue is whether it is in the interest of all that everyone should follow the rule. . . . In application, by contrast, the particular situation is relevant, regardless of whether general observance is also in the interest of all (as determined by the prior discursive examination). The issue here is whether and how the rule should be followed in a given situation in light of all of the particular circumstances. . . . What must be decided [in application discourse] is not the validity of the norm for each individual and his interests but its appropriateness in relation to all of the features of a particular situation.

In this way, Günther – and Habermas with him – hopes that moral norms can be both universal and effective in concrete situations. Application discourse takes some of the burden off the justification discourse because the latter is no longer burdened by the consideration of all the implications of the norm. At the same time, however, the application discourse also relativises the outcomes of the justification discourse because those outcomes are now no longer final.

Take for instance the norm 'you shall not lie'. Should this norm be applied rigorously and alike to all situations irrespective of the particulars of those situations? Here one can think of Kant's example of someone hiding a refugee in his home. What should the owner of the house do when the chasers of the refugee come knocking on the door, and the owner of the house knows that they will kill the refugee if they get hold of him? In this case we have a clash between two norms: the norm that 'you shall not lie' and a norm that says that you shall not kill or help in the killing of another person, and this is the kind of issue that application discourse is supposed to help solve.[6]

As mentioned, Habermas accepts the problem that Günther points to and he incorporates Günther's proposal into his discourse ethics. However, the division between justification and application raises a problem, which has most forcefully been pointed out by J. M. Bernstein (1995, 222–8). Application discourse is necessary because justification discourse is insufficient. The justification discourse cannot finish the job because it cannot consider every single situation, and there are always new situations which cannot be fully anticipated. The outcomes of justification discourse are, thus, open to re-interpretation in light of new circumstances (Habermas 1996a, 219). But then we may ask: what is the point of the justification discourse in the first place? What is the point of going through the justification discourse when its results can be overridden by the application discourse? Why not simply discuss and justify the norms in the concrete situations where they are supposed to be applied? Thereby we could do away with the seemingly superfluous justification discourse. That is, if the problem is the abstract nature of justification discourse, the solution may be to think of justification in a different way: as always embedded in a concrete form of life.

Of course, from a more strictly Kantian perspective, by incorporating Günther's application discourse into his discourse ethics, Habermas is giving up on deontology and caving into the Hegelian critique. This is so, it may be argued, when he carves out a role for application that makes application discourse constitutive, or defining, of moral norms. The danger, the argument would go, is that of contextualism and, thereby, moral relativism.

The Hegelian style critique is also reflected in two other kinds of critique of Habermas, however: that we should supplement the generalized other with a concrete other, and that Habermas's discourse ethics is at once too thin and too thick. These critiques are the subject of the following two sections.

CRITIQUE III: CONCRETE AND GENERALIZED OTHERS

Carol Gilligan (1982) is an American psychologist who has worked with and criticized Lawrence Kohlberg's theory of the moral and psychological development of children. Gilligan is critical of the idea of 'the generalized other', which she thinks does not fully capture what it means to be a moral person. Therefore she suggests that the generalized other must be supplemented by 'the concrete other'. The latter refers to an ethics of care and responsibility directed at concrete persons in concrete circumstances, where it is a matter of responding to the particularities of the other person and of the concrete circumstances of the situation. This ethics of care is characterized by the values of compassion and interdependence. Gilligan links the ethics of care to how women think morally, and she therefore believes that Kohlberg's and Habermas's theories of ethics are gender biased because they do not take this into consideration.

The critical theorist Seyla Benhabib (1986a, 339–42; 1986b) has taken up Gilligan's important critique and broadened it out in relation to Habermas. Benhabib associates the generalized other with universal rights and formal reciprocity and public institutions. And she associates the concrete other with the particular individuality of the other and what she calls complementary reciprocity, where different individuals complement one another in their particularities. With the concrete other, it is a matter of care and solidarity, and it is a matter of human individuality, not humanity. We must combine the two, Benhabib argues, and only if we do so, will discourse ethics provide an adequate theory of ethics. 'A communicative concept of autonomy', she writes,

> attains utopian and motivating force insofar as it promises neither a merger nor a fusion, but the necessary complementarity of these two perspectives. . . . Only then can we say that justice without solidarity is blind and freedom that is incompatible with happiness, empty. (Benhabib 1986a, 342)

So, Benhabib's proposal is that the moral perspective of discourse ethics must comprise both the generalized and the concrete other.

Only then can one do justice to the other, and only then can discourse ethics avoid being too abstract to be meaningful for real persons. Habermas in part takes on board Gilligan's and Benhabib's proposals. He believes that discourse ethics can include the perspective of the concrete other, because the moral perspective is supposed to consider *each* and every voice. And Habermas proposes that the idea of application discourse is doing just that because it considers the concrete circumstances of the application of a norm (Habermas 1993, 153f.; see also 1990, 175–81).

CRITIQUE IV: TOO LITTLE OR TOO MUCH?

Recall a point made earlier in the chapter: for Habermas, it is important that the participants in the discourse do not leave their interests, desires or particularities at the entrance to the discourse (p. 121). Rather, particular interests make up the raw material of discourse. It is, among other things, because of conflicts among different interests that the participants enter into discourse, and, once there, they discuss the universalizability of particular interests (is the student's wish to hand in his essay tomorrow compatible with a universalizable interest? And so forth). And importantly, only real flesh and blood persons can carry out the universalization test.

This gives rise to a critique of Habermas often levelled at Kant and at Kantian moral theories. The critique is that, because the moral perspective consists in an abstraction from everyday life, then a problem arises when we try to reconnect the results of the moral perspective (i.e. moral norms) with everyday life. The moral norms appear foreign or irrelevant to the concerns of real flesh and blood persons, who will then not be motivated to follow the moral norms. This problem is also referred to as the motivation problem. It can also be expressed as a simple question; 'Yes, but so what?' That is, the moral norms may be right and universal, but they must also be capable of motivating real persons.

Part of Habermas's response to the motivation problem is to insist that, although there is an element of abstraction in discourse, the participants in discourse are real persons who discuss real interests. As a result, there is less of a gap to bridge once we want to connect the outcomes of discourse to real life situations, and here the addition of application discourse can be seen as an extra way of bridging this gap.

To see why Habermas insists on this, it is useful to consider an aspect of his debate with the American Kantian political philosopher John Rawls (1921–2002) (Habermas 1998b, chapters 2–3; Rawls 1995; see also McCarthy 1994). Rawls (1971) believes that justice consists in abstracting from personal interests and from particular ways of life because these do not lend themselves to rational reconciliation. He conceives of the perspective of justice in terms of the original position where agents decide on the basic structure of society (the constitution, and so on) behind a 'veil of ignorance'. The point of the veil of ignorance is that the agents are not allowed to know their interests and their particular position within society. Only then, Rawls believes, will they be able to take a disinterested perspective and decide on the principle of justice. That is, only then will they be able to choose what is equally good for all.

But here is the problem from Habermas's perspective: what happens when the veil is gradually lifted and the agents consider the basic, and presumably just, structure of society in light of their own particular interests? The result is a potential clash between the result of the moral perspective behind the veil of ignorance and the perspective of the flesh and blood agents. In other words, potentially the real life agents will feel that justice is imposed on them from the outside, and if this is the case, then they are unlikely to be motivated to accept the norms and principles decided behind the veil of ignorance. This is why Habermas insists on the inclusion of real life persons and particularities within discourse. It is as a way to make sure that the agents will accept the norms for reasons that they find valid because they themselves have taken part in the process of giving reasons that constitutes the moral discourse.

These ways of connecting the generalized and the concrete, abstract morality and ethical life may constitute an answer to those who find Habermas's discourse ethics too abstract and 'thin'. As Habermas (1990, 207) writes:

[U]nless discourse ethics is undergirded by the thrust of motives and by socially accepted institutions, the moral insights it offers remain ineffective in practice. Insights, Hegel rightly demands, should be transformable into the concrete duties of everyday life. This much is true: any universalistic morality is dependent upon a form of life that *meets it halfway*.

However, this raises a different problem. If the moral point of view must be connected to particular interests and to a way of life, then the moral point of view – as conceived in Habermas's discourse ethics – may not be so 'thin' after all. This is a criticism of liberals and deliberative democrats that is often put forward by neo-Aristotelian and Hegelian communitarians such as Alasdair MacIntyre (1985; compare Habermas 1993, 95–105) and Charles Taylor (1994; compare Habermas 1993, 69–76; 1998b, chapter 8). Their critique – which may also apply to Habermas – is that, although the moral point of view claims universality, it is in fact only one (ethical) point of view among others. That is, although Habermas claims universality for discourse ethics, it is in fact just one perspective among others. Any perspective will be coloured by its particular context of emergence; it will be particular and interested. All we have are different ethical perspectives or conceptions of the good life, and so the distinction between the moral and the ethical is blurred or even disappears. So it may be argued that Habermas's discourse ethics is really the explication of a modern, pluralist and liberal democratic Western way of life. Its claim to universality is ideological in that it serves to hide the fact that actually it is just the expression of a particular way of life; and it is imperialistic because it is imposed on others in the name of universality. The communitarian critique is not exactly that discourse ethics is too 'thick' or insufficiently minimalist. Rather, the critique is that Habermas does not acknowledge that discourse ethics rests on a 'thick', ethical conception of the good life. In short, the critique is that Habermas does not acknowledge the particularity of the perspective of discourse ethics, which – from the neo-Aristotelian and communitarian perspective – is unavoidable.

From a different perspective, Habermas's discourse ethics (and his deliberative democracy) is too 'thick'. This is a critique that many liberals have of deliberative democrats like Habermas, and it also applied to Habermas's discourse ethics. The critique is that the Habermasian perspective rests on a particular conception of the person and of what constitutes a good society. The communitarian critique was similar, but the communitarians believe that this is necessarily so. Any theory of morality, justice, and so on, rests on a number of normative assumptions, for instance about the rationality of social agents. Therefore one must own up to this, which is what Habermas may be said not to do. From the perspective of liberalism, however, this is not necessarily so; from this perspective the problem is that Habermas has not rid his theory of these contentious assumptions. In short, from this perspective, it is possible to separate the moral perspective from ethical conceptions of the good life.

A variation of this critique is a critique put forward by Rawls (1995; response in Habermas 1998b, chapter 3). He argues that Habermas's discourse ethics (and his deliberative democracy) is metaphysical, which is a problem because a theory of justice should be only political and should only deal with political justice. It should be directed at political institutions and not rely on any conception of the person or any philosophy of language, which Rawls associates with metaphysics. A theory of justice must be free-standing in this sense; it must avoid these issues of the nature of language and so on. Habermas does not avoid these issues; on the contrary, he develops his ethics on the basis of, among other things, a theory of language.

Rawls believes that we do not need philosophy in this sense of metaphysics, and that it is of no use for a theory of justice, because it will only generate further disagreements. Habermas, on the other hand, believes that we cannot avoid doing philosophy and making assumptions about the person and about language. However, for Habermas, that is not a problem if it is done in the right way. Given the pluralism of modern societies, we can only come up with a procedural conception of justice, that is, a procedure for determining what is just. In other words, discourse ethics is, and must be, formalist. As opposed to this, Rawls provides a set of substantive principles of justice, that is, a set of substantive norms that should guide action and institutions. What is more, as we saw in Chapter 1, Habermas believes that philosophy should and can merely reconstruct universal structures of action, language and ethics. If this is the case, then philosophy is less dangerous and can provide potentially universal procedures. To conclude, both Habermas and Rawls believe that a theory of justice must be modest and not say too much, but they believe that the other is modest in the wrong way (Habermas 1998b, 72f.).

CONCLUSION

In the four previous sections, I have presented just four criticisms that have been levelled at Habermas's discourse ethics. There are many more, and, depending on one's interests, other criticisms may appear more important. As for the criticisms and Habermas's responses to them, it is up to the reader to make up his or her own mind. It is worth noting, however, that the criticisms presented here circle around the relationship between the concrete and the generalized, the ethical and the moral, and whether Habermas's discourse ethics is able to mediate the relationship between the two sides. This is an issue that goes back to, at least, Kant and Hegel, and more recently it has been the focus of debates in contemporary ethical and political theory, especially between communitarians and liberals and, most recently, around the issue of multiculturalism.[7] Habermas wants his discourse ethics to be deontological, cognitivist, formalist and universalist. In this, it is a very ambitious theory of ethics. What his critics are critical of may be seen as the ability of discourse ethics to cash in on these challenges to an ethics for modern, pluralist societies.

FURTHER READINGS

The most important among Habermas's texts dealing with discourse ethics are collected in two volumes: *Moral Consciousness and Communicative Action* ('Discourse Ethics' and 'Morality and Ethical Life') (1990) and *Justification and Application* ('On the Pragmatic, the Ethical, and the Moral Employments of Practical Reason' and 'Remarks on Discourse Ethics') (1993). J. M. Bernstein's *Recovering Ethical Life* (1995) contains an important and incisive critique of Habermas from another Critical Theory position. The edited volumes by Benhabib and Dallmayr (1990) and Rasmussen and Swindal (2002c) are the best volumes with critical assessments of Habermas's theory of ethics. The best longer introduction to, and discussion of, Habermas's discourse ethics is that of William Rehg (1997).

CHAPTER FIVE

DELIBERATIVE DEMOCRACY

INTRODUCTION

From the late 1980s onwards, Habermas (1988b; Appendices to 1996a) developed a theory of deliberative democracy. Habermas's (1996a) main work in legal and political theory, and the main focus of this chapter, is *Between Facts and Norms* with the revealing subtitle *Contributions to a Discourse Theory of Law and Democracy*, published in 1992 and translated into English in 1996. In later essays, Habermas has clarified and developed themes from this book (1998b; 2001b; 2006a, chapter 8), and he has taken the ideas in the direction of tolerance and religion, international law and cosmopolitan thought (2001b; 2006a; 2006b; 2008), which are the topics of the following chapter.

It would be a mistake to refer to these works as a 'political turn', however. As should be clear from the previous chapters, Habermas's earlier works were already political, even if they did not always address political institutions or practices. Habermas links his theories of communicative action and discourse ethics to the possibility of social critique and to the social integration of pluralist societies. In addition, he has addressed contemporary political issues in his so-called 'small political writings', of which *Time of Transitions* (2006a), *The Divided West* (2006b) and *Europe* (2009) are the most recent.

In many ways, Habermas's deliberative democracy is a continuation of his earlier work. First of all, deliberative democracy links the idea of the public use of reason to a theory of law and democracy where it is public deliberation, and hence the quality of the public sphere, that gives the laws their legitimacy. As such, *Between Facts and Norms* takes up themes from the early *The Structural Transformation of the Public Sphere* (1989a).

Moreover, we can think of deliberative democracy as a translation of the ideas developed in *The Theory of Communicative Action* (1984; 1987a) and 'Discourse Ethics' (in 1990) into the domain of politics. Recall that Habermas concluded that society can only be integrated peacefully in the long run if social integration is not reduced to instrumental action, but also involves communicative action, that is, action oriented towards mutual understanding (see Chapter 3). Recall also that normative validity is not a natural characteristic of the norm, but is an outcome of discourses among those affected by the norms. We can talk about what is normatively right, and we can do so in light of the rationality of the discourses about norms. Translated into the domain of politics, this means, first, that law cannot be reduced to legality or social facts, but must also have a dimension of legitimacy to them: we must be able to act not just instrumentally and strategically towards the law, but also out of respect for the legitimacy of the law. Second, it means that we can treat laws as legitimate insofar as we have arrived at them through discourses that are rational, which is to say characterized by inclusion, equality and sincerity in such a way that only the better argument will carry the day. This is, in essence, what Habermas purports to show with his discourse theory of law and democracy.

I shall first address the differences between morality and law and the need for law as a complement to morality in modern societies. I then place Habermas in relation to competing approaches to law and democracy and introduce his argument why law can, and must, be legitimate. Next I give an overview of Habermas's view of the political process that is supposed to lead to legitimate law, and I explain how this presents a solution to the problem of the colonization of the lifeworld encountered in Chapter 3. In the following section, I explain an important part of Habermas's deliberative democracy, namely the relationship between constitutionalism and democracy and what Habermas calls the basic system of rights. Finally, in order to illustrate Habermas's theory of deliberative democracy, I examine Habermas's writings on civil disobedience.

MORALITY AND LAW

Discourse ethics gave Habermas a way to account for the validity of moral norms, that is, for the moral bindingness of norms. However, morality alone cannot coordinate action in modern, complex societies.

Moral norms only have a weak motivational force, for instance through bad conscience; this is so especially in the impersonal contexts of strangers that characterize modern societies. However, law is backed by the coercive power of the state (including the police and the courts), and so law carries more motivational force in the impersonal relations among citizens in modern societies. Even if we do not follow the law out of conscience, we can be forced to follow it. For this functional reason, it is necessary to complement morality with law, according to Habermas (1996a, chapter 1, 104–18).

Another, related reason is the following. Habermas purports to show that law can be legitimate and that we can follow the law out of respect for it in the same way that we follow moral norms out of respect for them, because we take them to be legitimized in rational discourse or at least capable of such legitimation. However, this is not the whole story, because we can also relate instrumentally to the law. This is so even if we cannot relate purely instrumentally to the law in the long run for the same reasons that Habermas argued that we cannot act only instrumentally or strategically in the long run. If we did, it would become difficult, not to say impossible, to coordinate social action because we could not predict how others would react.[1] But, whenever we are faced with a particular law, we may approach it in an instrumental fashion and decide whether we act according to it or not on the basis of prudential reasons (risk of being caught, and so on) (ibid., 30). This adds a functional reason for the complementarity of law to morality in modern complex societies. The representatives of the law do not need to worry whether citizens follow the law out of respect for it, and the citizens are not burdened with the task of moral justification every time they face the law. We can bracket the question of the morality of a particular law, at least in the short run.

In short, then, law is efficient in a way that morality is not; or, in the terms of *The Theory of Communicative Action*, law can fulfil systemic aims that morality cannot. Indeed, according to Habermas (1996b, 1544), there are no alternatives to law: 'Law is the only medium through which a "solidarity with strangers" can be secured in complex societies.'

Law and morality differ in a number of ways. As we have seen, we can follow the law for both moral and prudential reasons. Law is enforced and positive, and we can follow it for both moral and prudential reasons. Unlike morality, law is backed by (state) violence, and law is positive in the sense that it is codified and enacted by a particular legal community. As a result of the positivity of the law, it only applies to everyone within a given polity or jurisdiction, which can be local, national, regional or global. That is, law applies to citizens or residents who are constituted as legal subjects by the law itself. This is in contrast to morality which is universal and applies to 'all' or 'everybody'. Finally, whereas morality applies to any domain, law leaves certain domains and issues unregulated. It is silent and indifferent about certain things that we would nonetheless consider a matter of morality, for instance lying to one's partner or being unfaithful to him or her.

In these ways, law and morality are different, but Habermas also links them through the discourse principle (D). The discourse principle, Habermas (1996a, 107) writes, 'lies at a level of abstraction that is *still neutral* with respect to morality and law, for it refers to action norms in general'. In *Between Facts and Norms* (ibid., 107), he defines the discourse principle thus: 'Just those norms are valid to which all possibly affected persons could agree as participants in rational discourses.' 'Action norms' can refer to both moral and legal norms. Insofar as we are dealing with moral norms, discourse ethics provide us with the universalization principle (U), where the criterion of validity is precisely the universalizability of the norm. In the case of law, the democratic principle reads: 'only those statutes may claim legitimacy that can meet with the assent (*Zustimmung*) of all citizens in a discursive process of legislation that in turn has been legally constituted' (ibid., 110). Below, I shall explain the way Habermas conceives of this process of validating legal norms. If we can talk about universalizability in the context of legal norms ('statutes'), it only refers to the 'universal' consent to those norms within a legally constituted polity, that is, among a particular set of legal subjects or citizens. The validity of legal norms is delimited in advance by the limits of the legal community. Nonetheless, as is the case with moral norms, it is (rational) discourse that bestows validity and legitimacy on legal norms. Thus, in the context of law, Habermas translates discourse ethics into a discourse theory of democracy – in short, a *deliberative* democracy.

LEGITIMATE LAW

Having settled the lack of alternatives to law as a medium of societal integration and the source of legitimate law in the democratic principle and the discourse principle, it remains to ask why we should choose a discourse theory of law and democracy over alternative approaches to law and democracy. How is deliberative democracy different from, and better than, other theories of law and democracy? As he is wont, Habermas develops his theory of deliberative democracy in critical dialogue with other theories. Here I shall only highlight some of the most important reasons why deliberative democracy may be better than the alternatives.

Habermas places himself and deliberative democracy in relation to other approaches to (1) law and (2) democracy.

(1) The German title of *Between Facts and Norms* is *Faktizität und Geltung*. Both titles reflect a central point that Habermas is making in the book, namely that we should neither reduce law to mere social facts nor subsume law to morality. That is to say, law is both fact and norm, both facticity and validity. Here Habermas (ibid., chapter 2) positions himself in contrast to the legal positivist and natural law traditions.

Thus, Habermas rejects legal positivism because it reduces law to social facts that one can only relate to in an instrumental or strategic fashion. According to Habermas, such a view precludes asking for the validity or legitimacy of legal norms; it reduces legal norms to legality and overlooks the dimension of legitimacy.

Niklas Luhmann's systems theory is one theory of law that reduces law to social facts (ibid., 47–51). Luhmann thinks of law as a system, where what matters is pragmatic success, and so law is removed from morality. The systems approach implies that the agents and the researcher take an observer's perspective on the law, judging its capacity to be an efficient means of systemic integration. In short, Luhmann treats the law as an object, as a social fact, which has nothing to do with morality; law and morality are different systems for Luhmann. Habermas (ibid., 43) refers to this view of law as 'the sociological disenchantment of law'. His point is that this view of law reduces law to something we can only describe as sociological facts and not something whose validity we can make reasoned judgements about.

Habermas is not only critical of legal positivism but also of the natural law tradition. The problem with the latter is that it reduces law to its moral content and thereby overlooks the positive nature of law, the fact that it is something made and backed by force. The natural law tradition also takes the bearers of natural law and rights to be pre-political beings; Locke is a good example of this position. But for Habermas this view misses an important aspect of the nature of law, namely that the legal subjects and bearers of rights are constituted as such by the law.

For Habermas, there are no rights that are natural in the sense of pre-political. For him rights are social; they are not rights that you have as an individual in isolation, but rights that you have as person whose personhood is constituted through social relations. This is the intersubjectivist perspective. Moreover, for Habermas, there can be no society without law, because morality is insufficient to integrate society on its own. So, we can neither go back to a state of nature nor go back to a society pre-existing government by law, whether in fact or in theory. Thus, rights are linked to law and to our status as citizens. They are linked to the fact that we are legal subjects as well as citizens engaged in law-making. If there are any basic rights, they are the rights that constitute us as free and equal under the law and as citizens capable of making our own laws.

All the same, Habermas believes that it is possible to speak of legitimacy and morality in relation to law. That is, and contra the legal positivists, he believes that law can have a 'moral' content; however, contra the natural law tradition, he believes that law cannot be subsumed to morality. Habermas's (ibid., 56–65) example of someone who subsumes law to morality is Rawls because Rawls hides the principle of justice behind the so-called veil of ignorance.[2] Accordingly, Habermas wants to steer a path between these two pitfalls of law as facticity and law as morality or natural law; or, rather, he wants to show that law can, and must, be both a matter of legality and legitimacy, facticity and validity. The theory of deliberative democracy is supposed to provide such a dual perspective on law and show how legality and legitimacy can be reconciled. That is, Habermas purports to show how one and the same law can be a social fact and be right, how we can follow it out of fear of reprisals and out of respect for its validity.

(2) In the context of democracy, too, Habermas (ibid., chapter 7; 1998b, chapter 9) wants to steer a path between reducing democracy to facticity and a utopian approach to democracy. Here he places himself between liberalism and republicanism.

Liberalism takes individuals as the starting point. The individuals have pre-political rights ('human' or 'natural' rights), and their identities and interests are formed prior to political deliberations.

Liberals conceive of rights as protection against the state and against the majority, that is, as negative rights from interference, and they typically conceive of politics as the aggregation of interests and votes. This sort of aggregative democracy, conceived on the model of the market, implies that the constitution should first of all contain individual liberty rights. As we have seen, Habermas is critical of the ideas of pre-political rights and pre-political identities and interests. He believes that liberals from Kant to Rawls tend to reduce democracy to a strategic game of maximizing one's interests and freedom to the negative freedom from interference from others.

Republicans, on the other hand, start from a common good: either the good of political activity where political participation is valued for its own sake, or a more substantive, communitarian good, say, a particular national tradition. Politics is conceived as a means for self-realization, either as the self-realization of our nature as political animals (as in Machiavelli and Rousseau) or of the good of the community (as in the communitarian thought of Alasdair MacIntyre [1985; Habermas 1993, 95–105] and Charles Taylor [1994; Habermas 1993, 69–76; 1998b, chapter 8]). Habermas argues that both views of politics are unrealistic today, the first because it requires too much in terms of political participation, which we cannot expect of citizens, and the second because of the pluralism of ethical conceptions of the good life (see also above in chapter 4, pp. 93–6). In terms of constitutional design, republicans would stress popular sovereignty and public autonomy as opposed to the constitutional rights and private autonomy of liberalism.

Habermas's (1996a, chapter 7; 1998b, chapter 9) alternative to the liberal and republican conceptions of democracy is to start from communication. He argues that the basic problem of both liberal and republican democratic thought is that they remain caught in what he calls the philosophy of the subject (see also above, chapter 1). The problem with liberals and republicans is that they start from an individual or collective subject, suggesting that the rationality and validity of laws can be decided with reference to those subjects' interests and identity (Habermas 1996a, 103). Liberals tend to start from individuals with given rights, identities and interests, thus making democracy a matter of maximizing one's self-interests; communitarians and republicans tend to take a collective identity as the starting point, thus making democracy a matter of realizing this already given collective identity.

As described in previous chapters, Habermas wants to substitute for the philosophy of the subject an intersubjectivist philosophy. His theory of deliberative democracy should be seen in this light as it shifts focus to the communication structures of society and to the quality of the public sphere and the discursive opinion and will formation. For him, democracy is more than the aggregation of already existing interests or the realization of an already existing communal identity. Rather, democracy has a formative role, and the deliberative process – from the public sphere to the parliament – is constitutive of interests and identities. Thus, the legitimacy of the laws is down to the quality of the deliberations about the laws, and, as we shall see in the following sections, this involves both individual rights and popular sovereignty, which Habermas thinks of as co-original.

FROM BULWARKS TO SLUICES

Recall Habermas's thesis of the colonization of the lifeworld in *The Theory of Communicative Action* (1987a, 357ff.) and his solution to build a bulwark around the lifeworld, protecting it against the system, including the spread of juridification (1997, 134–6; Chapter 3 above). He also referred to this as the 'siege' model for the protection of the lifeworld (1996a, 486f.).

In *Between Facts and Norms*, Habermas no longer uses the language of lifeworld, system and colonization in the same way and to the same degree. What is more important, *Between Facts and Norms* can be seen as a response to the colonization thesis and, especially, to the phenomenon of juridification, that is, the spread of positive law meant to secure freedom but effectively also limiting it. In *The Theory of Communicative Action*, the problem is that law is connected to system imperatives, and so the solution becomes to defend the lifeworld and communicative action against the law.

Between Facts and Norms presents a different and more positive solution. The solution is already foreshadowed in Habermas's (1987b, 364) earlier work, when he points to the importance of how the lifeworld and systems communicate with one another: 'it is a question of building up restraining barriers for the exchanges between system and lifeworld and of building in sensors for the exchanges between lifeworld and system'. Here the reference to 'barriers' point back towards the analysis in *The Theory of Communicative Action*, whereas the reference to 'sensors' point forward to the analysis and solution in *Between Facts and Norms*. In the latter work, Habermas proposes to root law in the communicative action of the lifeworld. This makes it possible to allow law back into the lifeworld without colonizing effects. It entails a different view of society and of the political process of law-making, however. Focus is no longer on the state (and the legislative, executive and judiciary) alone, but rather, and in line with the idea of a *discourse* theory of law and democracy, on the communication structures of society more generally.

Although the focus is not on any particular political institution, the public sphere nonetheless gains increasing importance. The public sphere is important as a sensor within the lifeworld, and Habermas (1996a, 360) describes it in the following way:

> The public sphere can best be described as a network for communicating information and points of view . . .; the streams of communication are, in the process, filtered and synthesized in such a way that they coalesce into bundles of topically specified *public* opinions.

The public sphere generates public opinion and a collective will, and it does so both through the aggregation of interests and through the discovery of a common identity.

The public sphere is anchored in the institutions of civil society. Habermas (ibid., 366f.) says of civil society that '[i]ts institutional core comprises those nongovernmental and noneconomic connections and voluntary associations that anchor the communication structures of the public sphere in the society component of the lifeworld'. Civil society is made up of 'more or less spontaneously emergent associations, organizations and movements' that have 'an egalitarian, open form of organization that mirrors essential features of the kind of communication around which they crystallize' (ibid., 367; see also Cohen and Arato 1992). Civil society should be distinguished from both state and market, and, although it is linked to the private sphere, it should also be distinguished from the latter (ibid., 367f.). Whether or not it is realistic to describe civil society as 'voluntary', 'egalitarian' and 'open', civil society is supposed to institutionalize those characteristics of discourse that are supposed to generate legitimacy. Habermas finds in civil society the societal resources for realizing something like a discursive or communicative democracy.

However, civil society cannot become a new centre of society. Habermas (ibid., 372) writes: 'Civil society can directly transform only itself, and it can have at most an indirect effect on the self-transformation of the political system; generally it has an influence only on the personnel and programming of this system.' Civil society can influence the political system, but cannot itself become the locus of political power. This is so because civil society is only a loose network of institutions and not a hierarchically organized institution. However, via the public sphere, civil society can translate communicative power into administrative power (ibid., 371). This takes us to Habermas's model of the circulation of power.

There is an 'official' and an 'unofficial' model of the circulation of power. In the official version, the public sphere provides inputs (opinions, votes and so on) into the parliamentary public sphere; the parliament makes laws; the executive executes those laws; and the judiciary gets involved in cases of conflict. This is how legitimate law and political authority are generated, and this is how things are supposed to be according to the self-understanding of constitutional democracies. In reality, however, power does not flow from the margins to the core, but in the opposite direction. This is the unofficial, unacknowledged version of the circulation of power. Here the public sphere is managed by the political parties and other political agents in the way Habermas described in *The Structural Transformation of the Public Sphere* (1989a). Furthermore, the parliament is dominated by the executive, and the result is that law is seen as alien and imposed on civil society and the lifeworld in the way Habermas described in *The Theory of Communicative Action* (1984; 1987a).

This rather bleak diagnosis of the circulation of power in contemporary democratic societies is tempered by the following qualification, however:

> I would like to defend the claim that *under certain circumstances* civil society can acquire influence in the public sphere, have an effect on the parliamentary complex (and the courts) through its own public opinions, and compel the political system to switch over to the official circulation of power. (Habermas 1996a, 373)

The aim, then, is to turn the unofficial circulation of power around, even if this is not always possible. Deliberative democracy is a way to do this, but note also the realistic element to Habermas's proposal: he does not believe that civil society and the public sphere can control the political system all the time. On the contrary, the normal state of affairs is characterized by the relative impotence of civil society and the public sphere.[3] The circulation of power can only be turned around 'in a perceived crisis situation' (ibid., 380) and not in routine situations when the agents of civil society are relatively passive. Habermas (ibid., 382–4) provides civil disobedience as one example of what may happen in crisis situations, and I shall return to this example at length in the last section of this chapter.

We can now go back to Habermas's strategy against the colonization of the lifeworld. As mentioned above, Habermas earlier thought it necessary to build a bulwark to protect the lifeworld against the colonization by the systems. In *Between Facts and Norms,* he suggests a different strategy, however. He now believes that it is possible to build 'sluices' to regulate the communication between the lifeworld and the systems and between civil society and the public sphere and the political system (ibid., 300, 354–6). The sluices can be opened in order for communicative power to flow into the political system: 'the procedures and communicative presuppositions of democratic opinion- and will-formation function as the most important sluices for the discursive rationalization of the decisions of an administration bound by law and statute' (ibid., 300; also 1998b, 250). The sluices can also be used to control the flow in the opposite direction. That is, they can be opened to let administrative power into civil society, but in a controlled manner so that civil society is not flooded by administrative power. In these ways – and even if it implies the acceptance of the state, of law and of system imperatives as permanent features of democratic politics – the sluice model for the relationship between lifeworld and systems is a less defensive response to colonization and juridification.

CONSTITUTIONALISM AND DEMOCRACY

Habermas (1996a, chapter 3) wants to take the best from liberalism and republicanism and combine them into his theory of deliberative democracy: individual rights (or constitutionalism) from liberalism and popular sovereignty (or democracy) from republicanism. The relationship between constitutionalism and democracy, individual rights and popular sovereignty is central to democratic theory, and has been so at least since Kant (liberalism) and Rousseau (republicanism). It is something that has occupied Habermas (1998b, chapter 10; 2006a, chapter 8) since the publication of *Between Facts and Norms.*

Today, constitutional democracy is almost the only game in town, and it is held by most people to be the best available form of government. It is also commonly thought that there must be a balance between constitutionalism and democracy, individual liberty rights and collective popular sovereignty, even if there is widespread disagreement about just what such a balance entails. Given that both constitutionalism and democracy are seen as essential, it is then a question of how exactly to balance the two and of whether one should enjoy priority over the other. The relationship between constitutionalism and democracy is important for a number of reasons, for instance the role of judicial review and the relationship between the courts and parliament; and, more abstractly, it is important for the relationships between the rule of law and popular sovereignty and between human rights and popular sovereignty.

To understand how Habermas thinks of the relationship between constitutionalism and democracy, it is necessary to go back to his conception of autonomy. The fundamental idea of Habermas's discourse ethics and deliberative democracy is autonomy understood as rational self-legislation, which is expressed in the principles of discourse and democracy. In the context of law, autonomy 'requires that those subject to law as its addressees can at the same time understand themselves as authors of the law' (Habermas 1996a, 120). Importantly, autonomy *qua* self-legislation must be rational in the sense that it must take place under certain idealized circumstances of equality, inclusion and so on. That is, autonomy should be understood as the citizens' free and equal deliberations about the laws that should govern their life together in the polity.

In the context of democracy, the idea of autonomy is that the people – the demos – give themselves their own laws. This is the republican insight with its emphasis on the self-legislation of the people. Yet, in order for autonomy to be *rational* self-legislation, the process must be regulated in such a way that, whatever the demos comes up with, everybody must be treated as free and equal citizens. This is the liberal insight with its emphasis on the protection of each individual's equal freedom. This is where constitutionalism enters into the picture, because it regulates who is to count as a participant in the law-making, what can be legislated and how. Typically, there will be constitutional rights protecting individuals' freedom of religion, which can then not be encroached upon by the majority.

Habermas's thesis is that, in order to ensure autonomy, the relationship between constitutionalism and democracy must be one of 'co-originality' (ibid., chapter 3; 2006a, chapter 8). Constitutionalism should not be imposed on democracy from the outside and in an arbitrary fashion, and democracy should not be seen as alien to constitutionalism. Habermas argues that, if considered in the right way, it is possible to think of constitutionalism and democracy as internally linked, as if they mutually imply one another. Constitutionalism and democracy are like a package deal: you need constitutionalism in order to make sure that everybody is free and equal under the law; and you need democracy in order that you can give yourself your own law, including constitutional law. You cannot have one without the other.

If you have both constitutionalism and democracy, then the addressees of the law will be able to see themselves as simultaneously the authors of the law: constitutional laws are not imposed on the citizens, but are the result of their own law-making, and their democratic law-making is regulated by constitutional law in such a way that everybody can have a free and equal say in the process. We do not first have a democratic process that generates constitutional laws, but instead we have a democratic process that must be constitutionally regulated in order to be legitimate. Nor do we first have a set of constitutional laws, because those laws must also be mediated by democratic opinion- and will-formation. Habermas argues that if we conceive of constitutional democracy along the lines of deliberative democracy, then this symbiotic relationship between constitutionalism and democracy can be realized. What is more, conceiving of constitutional democracy in this way guarantees freedom and equality: 'no one is truly free until all citizens enjoy liberties under laws that they have given themselves after a reasonable deliberation' (Habermas 2006a, 120).[4]

Habermas refers to the co-originality or 'co-implication' thesis as the thesis that constitutionalism and democracy are co-original or mutually imply and enable one another. The idea is that there is no constitutionalism properly speaking without democracy, and vice versa:

In a certain way, we consider both principles as equally original. One is not possible without the other, but neither sets limits on the other. The intuition of 'co-originality' can also be expressed thus: private and public autonomy require each other. The two concepts are interdependent; they are related to each other by material implication. (ibid., 114)

Constitutionalism and democracy are not mutually exclusive alternatives and are not competing sources of legitimacy. Strictly speaking, one cannot speak of constitutionalism without also implying democracy, and vice versa.

Recall that, for autonomy to be possible, the addressees of the laws must simultaneously be its authors. This condition extends to the laws of law-making, that is, to constitutional laws. However, in large and complex societies it is not possible to have this identity of addressees and authors, and this is so not just in the case of ordinary, day-to-day law-making but also in the case of constitutional law-making. The solution is representative democracy. The addressees must at least be able to understand themselves as also the authors of the law, even if they have not actually made the laws themselves. So the constitution must at least in theory be subject to democratic self-legislation, but this may take the form of representative democracy, where the citizens elect representatives to parliament or to a constitutional law-making body. That is, constitutional issues do not have to be the subject of day-to-day opinion- and will-formation. But ultimately the validity of laws – including the validity of the constitution – must be rooted in actual consent among those subject to the laws and not in a thought experiment as in Kant's monological legislator.

Constitutionalism must be mediated by democracy, but democratic law-making must also be regulated by constitutionalism, in particular in order to protect the pluralism of modern societies and to protect the integrity of the individual. In other words, only if the citizens are constituted as free and equal subjects under the law, will they be able to understand themselves as the authors of the law. For this reason the co-originality thesis holds that constitutionalism and democracy mutually imply and presuppose each other. The relationship between them is internal and enabling rather than external and constraining. The mediation of constitutionalism by democracy guarantees that constitutional rights are not paternalistically imposed on the demos, and the mediation of democracy by constitutionalism guarantees that the integrity of each individual is protected against the tyranny of the majority and that each individual has a free and equal voice in the process. Habermas concludes:

> [T]he idea of human rights is inherent in the very process of a reasonable will-formation: basic rights are answers that meet the demands of a political communication among strangers and ground the presumption that outcomes are rationally acceptable. The constitution thereby acquires the procedural sense of establishing forms of communication that provide for the public use of reason . . . Because this ensemble of enabling conditions must be realized in the medium of law, these rights encompass both liberal freedoms and rights of political participation. (ibid., 119)

In conclusion, then, Habermas's argument is that constitutionalism and democracy are co-original, and that we should not prioritize one over the other, which is what he believes that liberal and republican theorists have done since Kant (constitutionalism over democracy) and Rousseau (democracy over constitutionalism) (Habermas 1996a, chapter 3; see also Maus 2002). If anything comes first for Habermas, it is communication and discourse, and he views the relationship between constitutionalism and democracy through the communication or discourse perspective.[5]

This takes us to what Habermas (1996a, 82) calls the 'system of rights', which consists of 'the rights citizens must accord one another if they want to legitimately regulate their common life by means of positive law'. For Habermas (ibid., 118), the constitution is the specification of an abstract system of rights:

> [A] system of rights that gives *equal weight* to both the private and the public autonomy of citizens. This system should contain precisely the basic rights that citizens must mutually grant one another if they want to legitimately regulate their life in common by means of positive law.

The system of rights is supposed to capture both constitutionalism ('private autonomy') and democracy ('public autonomy'), and it is supposed to give equal weight to these. The system of rights is, then, what must be in place if the citizens are to be able to understand themselves as both authors and addressees of the laws. The system of rights expresses the co-originality of constitutionalism and democracy, individual rights and popular sovereignty insofar as the rights secure both at one and the same time.

Habermas specifies five categories of rights as making up the system of rights. The first three categories of rights define the citizens as 'free and equal persons' under law (ibid., 122), and it is important to stress that they are not natural or pre-political rights, but rights that one has as a member of a constitutional democracy. They secure the equal standing of citizens under the law. The three categories are: (1) basic rights 'to the greatest possible measure of equal individual liberties'; (2) membership rights in a voluntary association of equals, that is, the right to be a member of the polity on a free and equal basis; and (3) basic rights to 'individual legal protection' under the law (ibid., emphasis removed). Basically, these three categories of rights protect individual liberty or private autonomy, and they are associated with the liberal tradition. These three categories of rights are mainly aimed at the citizens' roles as addressees of the law, and even if they are listed first, they do not enjoy priority over the fourth category of rights, which is aimed at the citizens' roles as authors of the law: (4) 'Basic rights to equal opportunities to participate in processes of opinion- and will-formation in which citizens exercise their political autonomy and through which they generate legitimate law' (ibid., 123, emphasis removed). The fourth category of rights consists of political rights of participation in the law-making process, and, as such, they protect citizens' public autonomy. They are associated with the republican tradition. Together, the first four categories of rights express the co-originality of constitutionalism and democracy because they secure both private autonomy (i.e. individual liberty) and public autonomy (i.e. popular sovereignty).

While the first four categories of rights are 'absolutely justified categories of civil rights' (ibid.), the fifth category of rights is relative to the first four in that it is necessary in order to realize the first four categories of rights. The fifth category of rights contains: (5) 'Basic rights to the provision of living conditions that are socially, technologically, and ecologically safeguarded, insofar as the current circumstances make this necessary if citizens are to have equal opportunities to the civil rights listed in (1) through (4)' (ibid.). That is, although necessary in the present, these social rights enjoy a relative and secondary status vis-à-vis the rights that secure private and public autonomy. Social rights are necessary for, but also derivable from, individual liberty and political freedom.

AN EXAMPLE: CIVIL DISOBEDIENCE

In this section, I shall present Habermas's (1985; 1996a, 382–4) views on civil disobedience.[6] This is not because civil disobedience is central to his theory of deliberative democracy, but only because Habermas's treatment of the issue of civil disobedience highlights some important themes in his theory of deliberative democracy. Habermas's view of civil disobedience throws up issues in relation to the role of civil society and the public sphere vis-à-vis the political system; in relation to the role of constitutional principles and public deliberation; and in relation to the relationship between constitutionalism and democracy.

The specific context of Habermas's (1985) main writings on civil disobedience was the protests against the deployment of nuclear missiles by the United States in West Germany in 1983. In his writings on civil disobedience, Habermas draws on the American experience of the civil rights movement and the protests against the Vietnam War in the 1960s and 1970s, and he also draws on Rawls's (1971, 363–91) comments on civil disobedience. Like Rawls, Habermas believes that civil disobedience should not be reduced to a matter of legality or of law and order, but should rather be treated as a matter of political culture. Civil disobedience, Habermas says, is part of a thriving civil society and public sphere, because it is a way for the citizens to turn around the circulation of power. And Habermas argues that, like the United States, West Germany had a mature political culture so that it was possible to be tolerant towards acts of civil disobedience.

Habermas's definition of civil disobedience is interesting for what it reveals of his theory of deliberative democracy. He understands an act of civil disobedience on the model of a public argument, and civil disobedience should be understood as an extension of public deliberation. Civil disobedience is part of what Habermas (1996a, 307) refers to as the 'wild' public, that is, the unorganized networks of communication and action outside the formal political system. It is part of a healthy civil society and public sphere, and should be seen as a normal and valuable phenomenon, albeit within certain limits to which I return shortly. This is so because it acts as a sensor in civil society for signs that the law is illegitimate – in short, it acts as a sign of legitimation crisis, and it can be the starting point for turning the unofficial circulation of power around.

Thus, for Habermas, acts of civil disobedience should, first, be non-violent and symbolic acts as distinguished from, for instance, acts of terrorism. Here one may also think of Habermas's comments on the student protests in the late 1960s in West Germany, examined at the end of Chapter 2. Habermas (1981, 306) criticized the students for their 'pure actionism'. His problem with the student protests was that the students tended to aestheticize action and to pursue civil disobedience for its own sake in a kind of fetishism of action. Thus, the problem with the student protests was that they did not always pursue civil disobedience as arguments in a public debate about the future of the university or as a strategy for provoking debate and not just a violent reaction by the system).

An act of civil disobedience should, second, be an appeal to the majority's sense of justice; that is, it should be a public argument with the aim of influencing public opinion and, eventually, the lawmakers. For that reason, civil disobedience should not seek to further private interests or conceptions of the good life – it should, rather, appeal to justice, to what is right. As an argument, civil disobedience should appeal to everybody. Third, civil disobedience should only be used as a last resort and in cases of grave injustice, and it must appeal to the principles of constitutional democracy, that is, the system of rights that Habermas reconstructs in *Between Facts and Norms.*

To be justified, civil disobedience must be non-violent or symbolic and the civil disobedient must be able to justify her act with reference to constitutional principles. In addition, it must be a last resort in that the civil disobedient must have exhausted all legal routes, and she must be ready to accept the legal consequences of her act, even if Habermas believes that the courts can show leniency in these cases. The latter conditions are important because civil disobedience challenges the law, even if it does not amount to revolution. According to Habermas, it cannot be reduced to legality, but is situated somewhere between legality and legitimacy, between facts and norms. Legality does not exhaust legitimacy, and the act of civil disobedience appeals to something beyond the law, namely the public's sense of justice and the principles of constitutional democracy.

However, law is essential for the integration of modern societies, and the act of civil disobedience should not endanger the legal order as a whole. Although civil disobedience cannot be judged on its (il)legality alone, we cannot dismiss of the dimension of legality when judging the act of civil disobedience; after all, we cannot do without law and a legal system in a modern, complex society. As a result, we must judge both the legality and the legitimacy of an act of civil disobedience. Civil disobedience, Habermas (1985, 106) writes, is 'suspended between legality and legitimacy' because both of these are essential components of constitutional democracy. Although Habermas prioritizes legitimacy over legality in respect of particular laws, he does not consider civil disobedience as a matter of either legality or legitimacy. This corresponds to the idea that law can be reduced to neither legality (facticity) nor legitimacy (morality).

To go back to the deployment of American nuclear missiles in West Germany in the early 1980s, Habermas believes that civil disobedience was justified in that case. Civil disobedience is not justified with reference to the outcome of a decision making procedure, but with reference to the fairness of the procedure. This point about civil disobedience corresponds to a larger point of discourse ethics and deliberative democracy. We cannot say what the right decision or a valid law is independently of the procedure we have followed in order to arrive at it; it is the rationality of the procedure that determines if the outcome is fair: has everybody potentially affected been included? Did everybody have an equal say in the process? And so on.[7]

In the case of the nuclear missiles there was a problem with the procedure for arriving at the decision. The decision was made with a simple majority in the West German parliament. However, Habermas argued that the deployment of the missiles posed such an extreme threat that it required the consent of everybody affected. What is more, the citizens must be able to see themselves as part of the same 'we', and this was missing in this case because there was no common political culture, because alternative political (sub)cultures had developed in West Germany. The problem arises when pluralism cuts so deep that the minority cannot accept the outcome of the majority rule, for instance because the minority is afraid that it will always be in the minority. Another reason why the decision by majority rule was unjustified was that the decision was irreversible, which makes it impossible for a minority to change the decision at a later point in time (ibid., 110f.).[8] Although Habermas believes that majority rule is a permanent feature of constitutional democracy, some decisions must not be taken by majority rule. If they nonetheless are, this may justify the use of civil disobedience.

In sum, Habermas's definition of civil disobedience involves a qualified justification of civil disobedience: civil disobedience is justified if it is mediated by the public use of reason, by the principles of constitutional democracy and by the legal order as a whole. In other words, although civil disobedience is a challenge to the existing order, there are certain things that cannot be challenged, namely the public use of reason as the source of legitimacy, the basic system of rights and law as the medium of societal integration in modern societies.

The example of civil disobedience shows how, for Habermas, deliberative democracy combines facts and norms, legality and legitimacy, when it comes to law and democracy. Furthermore, it show how, for Habermas, the source of legitimacy is the public use of reason, and that administrative power should be rooted in the communicative power of civil society and the public sphere, as is the case in the official model of the circulation of power. In short, the example of civil disobedience shows the importance of the ability of the addressees of the law to see themselves simultaneously as the authors of the law. Civil disobedience is only justified when this is not the case, that is, where the citizens feel alienated from the law and from the political system.

CRITIQUE I: CIVIL DISOBEDIENCE, CONSTITUTIONALISM AND DEMOCRACY

In continuation of the preceding section, I want to raise two issues in the context of Habermas's conception of civil disobedience, two issues with wider implications for his theory of deliberative democracy. The first issue concerns the relationship between constitutionalism and democracy (1), and the second the relationship between the constitutional principles and democratic action (2).

(1) Although Habermas draws on Rawls in his writings on civil disobedience, the emphasis on the public sphere may point to a difference in Rawls's and Habermas's respective conceptions of law and democracy. Habermas puts relatively more emphasis on civil disobedience as an argument in the public sphere, and Rawls stresses the appeal to the principles of justice that are determined behind the veil of ignorance in the original position. For Rawls, and contrary to Habermas, civil disobedience is first and foremost an appeal to an already defined concept of justice and a way to defend this concept of justice against majority decisions.

Habermas wants to reconcile constitutionalism and democracy, but the case of civil disobedience throws up the question whether such reconciliation is possible at all. The civil disobedient must appeal to the principles of constitutional democracy, but what do you do if the constitution is imperfect or if it has not been properly mediated by the rational self-legislation of the citizens? The fact that civil disobedience may be necessary may precisely be a sign that the basic system of rights is not fully in place or that not all citizens agree on what those basic rights should be. This is also a problem if we bracket the appeal to constitutional principles and only focus on the role of civil disobedience as a public argument. In order for the public use of reason to be the source of legitimate law it must be regulated by something like the constitutional principles, guaranteeing equality, full inclusion and so on. However, if these principles are not in place, then the appeal to the public's sense of justice seems equally impotent: what guarantees that the public will pay attention to an argument for justice?

Thus, while Habermas sees civil disobedience as an important part of a political system where the laws are not fully legitimate – that is, as part of an imperfect constitutional democracy where constitutionalism and democracy are not fully reconciled – it seems that just this imperfectness makes it difficult for civil disobedience to function in the way Habermas thinks it should, namely as an appeal to the majority's sense of justice and to the principles of constitutional democracy. Put slightly differently, if the system of rights is not fully in place and if the public sphere is distorted (because of colonization by the market and the state), then civil disobedience may be necessary. However, this is also the kind of situation where there is no straightforward way of deciding whether civil disobedience is justified because we then do not have any stable foundation to fall back upon, whether a clear system of rights or the forceless force of the better argument.

Is that a problem for Habermas? That depends on how you read him. If you read him as someone who wants to draw clear distinctions between legitimate and illegitimate political action, then the ambiguity of civil disobedience is a problem for him. However, if you read Habermas as someone who is sensitive to the value of 'wild' publics and critical of the conservative law and order mentality, then the ambiguity of civil disobedience is not such a big problem and may even be seen as part and parcel of a thriving democracy.

(2) The second issue that arises from Habermas's view of civil disobedience concerns the status of the principles of constitutional

democracy, that is, the system of rights. The question here is whether these principles or rights are something that the citizens should discover or whether they are something the citizens themselves construct. In other words, are the principles or rights already defined and only await our discovery of them, or should we rather think of them as something to be defined through political action.

Take, for instance, the following quote from the discussion of civil disobedience in *Between Facts and Norms* (1996a, 384):

> [T]he justification of civil disobedience relies on a *dynamic understanding* of the constitution as an unfinished project. From this long-term perspective, the constitutional state does not represent a finished structure but a delicate and sensitive – above all fallible and revisable – enterprise, whose purpose is to realize the system of rights *anew* in changing circumstances, that is, to interpret the system of rights better, to institutionalize it more appropriately, and to draw out its contents more radically. This is the perspective of citizens who are actively engaged in realizing the system of rights. Aware of, and referring to, changed contexts, such citizens want to overcome in practice the tension between social facticity and validity.

From the first part of the quote, it would seem that the process of materializing the system of rights is an open-ended process of defining what the system of rights should consist in, with no guarantee what the result will be. The system of rights may be given, but it is so abstract that it needs to be interpreted in order to have any meaning at all. Hence why Habermas refers to this process as 'dynamic' and 'revisable'. In the second part of the quote, however, the picture changes. Here it would seem that the system of rights is already defined and merely needs to be institutionalized 'more appropriately'; here it is a matter of discovering what the system of rights entails and then realize it in practice.

These two views of the relationship between the principles of constitutional democracy, or the system of rights and political action, characterize much of Habermas's political philosophy. There is a tension – or oscillation – between the view that political action consists in discovering and realizing the principles or rights and the view that political action consists in constructing and determining these principles and rights. The two views rest on different views of the status of the principles or rights (already defined or yet to be defined) and the status of political action (secondary to or constitutive of the principles and rights). Thus, on the first view, civil disobedience is part of an attempt to realize more fully an already defined set of principles and rights; on the second view, it is part of an open-ended and non-teleological process of political action (Thomassen 2007, chapter 4). In terms of constitutionalism and democracy, the question is what the role of democracy is in relation to constitutionalism: is it to materialize constitutional rights already there waiting for us to discover them, or does democracy have a more constructive and defining role?[9] The first option would be the 'liberal' one, the second the 'republican' one.

CRITIQUE II: DELIBERATION AND INCLUSION

It should be clear by now that the rationality of deliberation depends on their inclusiveness. We can think of inclusiveness in two ways, both of which are essential to deliberative democracy. There is, first, the inclusion into deliberation. This is what Habermas refers to when he uses expressions such as 'all those possibly affected' by a moral or legal norm. Here it is a matter of who is allowed a say in the deliberations. Second, there is the inclusion which is, in a sense, internal to deliberation. This is what Habermas refers to when he stipulates conditions of deliberation such as equality and full information. Here it is not simply a matter of (formal) access to the deliberations, but of the conditions under which citizens can have a say in the deliberations. We can imagine that everybody is formally included into the deliberations (even if only indirectly through representation), but that not everybody has an equal say within the deliberations.

This is a critique that several authors have put forward against Habermas (see, for instance, Norval 2007). The critique is that Habermas's conception of deliberation is a restrictive one because it relies on a certain notion of what it means to be rational, what it means to give rational arguments and so on. Thus, the critics argue that, even if Habermas allows everybody to have a voice in the making of law, in reality some are more equal and have more voice than others because they rational or are rational in the right way.

Iris Marion Young is one of those who have criticized Habermas on this account. According to her, deliberative democracy – including Habermas's version of it – usually rests on particular conceptions of what it means to deliberate and to be rational, and that these go unacknowledged in deliberative democratic theory. She writes: 'The model of deliberative democracy tends to assume that deliberation is both culturally neutral and universal' (Young 1996, 123, see also 1990, chapter 4). Legitimate law is law that has passed the test of the better argument, but Young points out that what 'argument' and 'reason' are is a contested matter. Argumentation and reasoning may take different forms of which Habermasian deliberation is only one. As a result, we need 'a more inclusive model of communication' (Young 1996, 123). A more inclusive democracy is one that takes the plurality of ways of arguing and reasoning into consideration and allows for different modes of partaking in deliberations (which are then strictly speaking not deliberations, but something broader). The latter include rhetoric, narratives and the activist politics of civil disobedience (Young 2000, chapter 2; 2001), and this inclusion of a wider array of voices is a response to the pluralism of contemporary societies.

Whether or not her own alternative to Habermasian deliberative democracy overcomes the problems she identifies in Habermas's deliberative democracy, it is useful to look briefly at her proposal. She proposes a theory of 'communicative democracy', where 'communicative' captures the wider notion of ways of participating in deliberations. She writes that it involves

> equal privileging of any forms of communicative interaction where people aim to reach understanding. While argument is a necessary element in such an effort to discuss with and persuade one another about political issues, argument is not the only mode of political communication, and argument can be expressed in a plurality of ways, interspersed with or alongside other communicative forms. (Young 1996, 125)

A communicative democracy only rests on 'a norm of reasonableness, which is a general norm of communicative action that aims to reach understanding' (Young 2000, 38). Further, communicative democratic action takes place within 'agreed-upon and publicly acknowledged procedures' (ibid., 110). In the terms of this chapter, Young's critique is that the citizens can only see themselves as both addressees and authors of the law if they are excluded neither directly nor indirectly. In order for that to be the case, one must be aware of hidden exclusions in the way we think about deliberation and communication, and so deliberative democracy must reflect on what constitutes deliberation and communication (more critically Gould 1996).

Notice that, although Young (2000, 12) wants to extend the range of 'styles and terms of debate', including civil disobedience, she argues for this from a starting point similar to that of Habermas, namely communicative reason. Thus, although critical of Habermas's theory of deliberative democracy, she is so from a position within Critical Theory. In other words, although Habermas's theory of deliberative democracy is based in the Critical Theory tradition, it is not the only theory of democracy – or even deliberative democracy – that may come out of this tradition (see also Bohman 2000; Chambers 1996; Dryzek 2000; Fraser 1997).

FURTHER READINGS

Habermas's *Between Facts and Norms* is written in a systematic fashion, but is also a difficult read. The best place to start is the Postscript and Appendices to that book and some of the essays in *The Inclusion of the Other* (Part V) and in *Time of Transitions* (chapter 8). For useful discussions of Habermas's theory of deliberative democracy, the best volumes are Deflem (1996), Rosenfeld and Arato (1998), von Schomberg and Baynes (2002) and Rasmussen and Swindal (2002b). Bohman and Rehg (1997) contains good discussions of deliberative democracy more generally. Other deliberative theorists who share some, but not all, of Habermas's views include Bohman (2000), Chambers (1996) and Dryzek (2000). For a good overview of theories of deliberative democracy, see Held 2006, chapter 9. Critics of Habermas include Fraser (1997), Mouffe (2000), Norval (2007) and Young (1990).

CHAPTER SIX

THE NEW POLITICAL CONSTELLATION

INTRODUCTION

This chapter rounds up and rounds off this introduction to the work of Jürgen Habermas by examining three issues that have been the focus of Habermas's work during the time since the publication of *Between Facts and Norms* in 1992. The first issue is captured by a phrase used by Habermas – 'the post-national constellation' – to refer to the need to move beyond the nation-state. Thus, in the first section, I will deal with Habermas's writings on Germany, Europe and cosmopolitanism. The second issue could be described as 'the post-secular constellation', and in the second section I shall deal with Habermas's writings on religion, secularism and tolerance. Finally, the third issue could be described as the new constellation of human nature, and here I will deal with Habermas's writings on human cloning and new biotechnologies which change our relation to nature, including our own nature. While the first two issues can be seen as applications and developments of the theory of deliberative democracy, the third issue touches more on communicative rationality and discourse ethics. Together, the three issues make up a new political constellation, which Habermas seeks to respond to through the lenses of his theories of communication, ethics and democracy.

THE POST-NATIONAL CONSTELLATION

The problem of the nation-state

According to himself, the experiences of Nazism and the Holocaust led Habermas to be suspicious of any actual or potential totalitarianism.

The same experiences may be the sources of his sceptical attitude vis-à-vis nationalism, which was, after all, an essential part of Nazism.

These concerns of Habermas came to the fore during the 1980s and 1990s. There was, first, the so-called 'historians' debate' (*Historikerstreit*) in Germany in the mid-1980s (Habermas 1989b, chapters 8–9; Holub 1991, chapter 7). The debate concerned both the present and the past and especially the use of the past in the present. Conservative historians argued for a sort of normalization of the German Nazi past. They did not argue that the Holocaust had not taken place or any such thing, but they made two important claims: first that contemporary (West) German society should no longer feel burdened by the Nazi past, and, second, that the Holocaust could be compared to the Soviet gulag. In both cases, the result is normalization: (West) Germany is like other countries and can act like other countries. The latter was important for those – mainly conservatives – who wanted to see a greater role for (West) Germany in world politics.[1]

Habermas too believed that (West) Germany should become a player in the world, but not as a nation, only as a democratic state. Like other leftist and liberal intellectuals, Habermas responded to the conservative historians by saying that their normalization of German history was an attempt to make short-term gains in elections and in public opinion. Habermas also argued – as he also did in the later debate about a memorial for the victims of the Holocaust (Habermas 2006a, chapter 4) – that, although the past is past and must be treated as such, it forms part of who we are as a collective, for instance as a nation. Or, to be more precise, the way we relate to the past forms part of, and define, who we are and who we want to be as a collective. Thus, for Habermas, the break in 1945 was important and must be understood as liberation and not as defeat. Habermas again and again stresses that Germany should orient itself towards the western intellectual tradition, which includes constitutional democracy (Habermas 1989b, chapter 10; 1997, 100–3). In other words, Nazism was a part of the German past, but one whose ideas and practices must be repudiated in order that Germany can continue on a different path in the future, a path that includes the principles of the French and American Revolutions and the principles of constitutional democracy.

Three things are important here. First, the past is important as future, to paraphrase Habermas (1994). That is, what is particularly important about history and memorials is how they become part of a critical collective self-reflection and self-transformation. Thus, Habermas (2006a, 44) writes in the context of the memorial for the victims of the Holocaust that 'the goal of the memorial is to challenge future generations to take a stand, to take a stance on what the memorial expresses, what Auschwitz meant for German identity a half century after the event'. Thereby also said, second, that this self-reflection must, for Habermas, be public. For instance, a memorial should be seen as a contribution to and catalyst of public deliberation about the past and the future of the collective (Habermas 1997, chapters 1–2; 2006a, chapter 4). And, finally, Habermas's position suggests that the nation is not some natural entity, and that what relates a collective to its past and to one another is not blood. Rather, nations are political constructs, and what constitutes the nation – or the polity – is the public deliberations about who we are and who we want to be, that is, ethical deliberations that take their object – namely, collective identity – as a project to be embarked upon rather than as fate.

This leads me to make three more systematic points about Habermas's view of the nation-state. First of all, the nation and the nation-state are not natural and ahistorical entities. Rather, they have a history and emerge at a particular point in (European) history in response to developments in the European societies. Very briefly, that nation provided the glue that provided solidarity among citizens in modern states. Thus, neither the nation nor the (modern) state is a natural phenomenon; both are political achievements that once did not exist and that may some day cease to exist and cease to appear to be the natural units for politics and democracy.[2] This is important because it suggests that the nation-state is not a given and that it may not be the only or the best solution to the problems facing us today or in the future.

Second, Habermas also believes that the relevant unit for a political collective is not an ethnos but a demos. It is neither blood nor ethnicity, culture, religion or language that provides the glue of solidarity. Habermas does not deny that these things may be important to many people, but he argues that, as far as the polity goes, they should not define the polity. Instead, the relevant collective is the demos – the people as a demos, that is, as a collective that defines itself through democratic processes of which the opinion- and will-formation of the public sphere is an essential part. Democratic self-determination does not consist in the expression of an already existing, pre-political and 'natural' identity of the people, but in the active creation of the identity of the people. '*Citizens* constitute themselves on their own as a political association of the free and equal; *Volksgenossen* see themselves as belonging to an ethnic community bound together by a common language and historical destiny' (Habermas 1997, 173).

What is important is that the citizens subscribe to more or less the same political and democratic values and to the democratic procedures, which include individual rights to protect the right to be different. If we should at all speak of a 'nation', then it should be the nation as a demos and not as an ethnos. This solves the problems that the state is often made up of different ethni, and that the nation *qua* ethnos often straddles different states. The non-identity between state and nation, and between society and nation is covered over by the fiction of the nation-state. However, it is just that: a fiction, because state and nation are not linked by necessity, only by historical contingency.

However, third, the nation-state is increasingly under threat today. It is under threat from within and from without. From within, the nation-state is under threat from immigration and from the increasing national, ethnic and religious self-awareness of minority groups. These developments serve to undermine the unity of the nation-state as a one-nation (*qua* ethnos) state. Sometimes it results in claims to secession or autonomy as in Ex-Yugoslavia and Canada; sometimes it results in claims for special rights to, for instance, language education. In both cases, the claims challenge the identity between ethnos and demos, nation and state.

From without, the nation-state is under threat from what is usually just referred to as globalization. Globalization can take many forms, for instance linguistic and cultural forms. Most important for Habermas is economic globalization, which puts pressure on the welfare state, especially because of the limits to the ability of the state to raise taxes. The problem is manifold: there is increasing interdependence among the nation-state economies so that one country is limited by other countries' actions; multinational companies gain increasing powers and can move capital and production from one country to another; and so on. All in all, these developments limit the state's ability to control its own destiny, whether in the area of foreign policy or in the area of taxation. For Habermas, these developments suggest that we need to look for ways of institutionalizing regional and global polities. I shall present Habermas's proposal in this regard below, but first I turn to his solution to the first threat against the nation-state, namely the threat to the unity of the demos as an ethnos.

Beyond the *nation*-state

Habermas has three responses to the problems of the unity – or lack thereof – of the unity of the *nation*-state where the people is understood as an ethnos. The first response is to emphasize democracy (1); the second is to make a distinction between the ethical and the political (2); and the third is the notion of constitutional patriotism (3).

(1) I have already touched upon the importance of democracy, both in this and in the previous chapter on Habermas's theory of deliberative democracy. In brief, any polity should be a democratic one and democracy should be the principle according to which its basic matters are organized. Thus Habermas emphasizes the democratic procedures, including the role of the public sphere, and he emphasizes the role of democratic values and the political culture in integrating a pluralist society. The identity of the polity – and of the people, the demos – must be mediated by democratic opinion- and will-formation. At the same time, everybody should enjoy equal rights, which consist of both individual freedom rights and political rights of participation in the making of the laws (cf. also 'the system of rights'). Only in this way can everybody take part in the formation of the identity of the people and the polity and do so freely and equally.

Habermas's views on the German reunification in 1989/90 illustrate this view of democracy and the identity of the people. The debate about German reunification is linked to other debates about German history and identity, including the 'historians' debate' and the debate about the Holocaust memorial mentioned above. Habermas's views on reunification exemplify well his view that democracy must be a central part of any response to the fact that the state cannot fall back upon an ethnos.

Habermas was critical of the way reunification happened. His main objection was a procedural one, albeit one with a wider bearing. West Germany's 'Basic Law' contained two articles – Articles 23 and 146 – both of which could be used as the constitutional basis for reunification, but with different implications. Article 23 allowed 'other parts' of Germany to join West Germany without any changes to the constitution (i.e. the 'Basic Law'). Article 146 treated the 'Basic Law' as merely provisional, the idea being that the Germans would later constitute themselves with a proper constitution (remember that the 'Basic Law' was given to the West Germans by the then occupiers after World War II). In the event, the conservative West German government used Article 23, and the reunification took the form of an administrative annexation. Habermas believed that Article 146 would have been better. Referring to the reunification, he writes, that it 'dishonestly evades one of the essential conditions for the founding of any nation of state-citizens: the public act of carefully considered democratic decision taken in both parts of Germany' (Habermas 1992c, 96; see also 1994, 33–54; 1997, 95–105).[3] The reason for this view should be clear by now. Who we are as a political collective, and how we organize our lives together, should be the subject of democratic opinion- and will-formation. It should not be handed down to us from the past and should not be given by some blood-based community of fate, and it should not be a merely administrative matter as if it were merely a matter of pragmatic efficiency.

(2) Democracy is one part of Habermas's response to the non-identity between nation and state. Another important part of his response is a distinction between ethical and political societal integration. Here it is necessary first to go back to the distinction from Habermas's discourse ethics between pragmatic, ethical and moral perspectives on practical questions (cf. above pp. 93–6). Recall that the ethical perspective concerns what is good for me or for us, that is, what is good relative to the history or way of life of a particular subject. The moral perspective concerns what is equally good for all (i.e. what is right), and so it is not relative to any particular point of view. In discourse ethics, the moral perspective trumps the ethical perspective in cases of conflict between the two perspectives. More generally, Habermas's discourse ethics is primarily concerned with moral autonomy – that is, with moral, rational self-legislation – than with ethical self-expression. Ethical reasons are not neutral vis-à-vis the ethical pluralism of modern societies. The moral perspective is not neutral either, because it is informed by the concept of autonomy as rational self-legislation, but it is supposedly neutral in relation to different ethical conceptions of the good.

The distinction between ethical and moral reasons forms the background for the distinction Habermas makes between ethical and political reasons or forms of societal integration (1996a, 104–18; 1998b, chapter 8; 2004; and Bernstein 1996 for a critique). His argument is that, because of the pluralism of modern societies, we must distinguish between two levels: the level of the ethical with the pluralism of ethical conceptions of the good and the level of the political consisting of democratic and constitutional principles and procedures. Because of the pluralism of ethical conceptions of the good, society cannot be integrated on the basis of a single ethical conception of the good life, at least not without imposing this on those who do not share this particular conception of the good life. As a consequence, it is necessary to integrate society at the level of the political; that is, what citizens within a society must share is not a particular way of life, but allegiance to a common political culture.

If we conceive of society along these lines, it is possible to include groups and individuals with different ways of life and to do so in an unbiased way. 'Inclusion', Habermas (2001b, 73) writes, 'means that the political community stays open to include citizens of any background without confining those *Others* within the uniformity of a homogeneous national community'. Demos, not ethnos. Only if the political culture remains distinguished from and neutral vis-à-vis the ethical conceptions of the good, only then can the political culture include the different conceptions of the good. Political reasons trump ethical ones; that is, the political enjoys priority over the ethical. If the political level is distinguished from the ethical level in this way, it is possible to include different ways of life in an equal fashion.

The ethical–political distinction is important when it comes to the question of immigration. Here Habermas argues that the inclusion or exclusion of immigration cannot be based on ethical reasons, and he argues that what is demanded of immigrants should be political and not ethical acculturation. That is, immigrants must become part of the demos; their inclusion into the ethnos of the nation is irrelevant for their status as citizens and rights bearers. This is an argument that Habermas (1998b, 226–36) makes most forcefully in the context of immigration debates in Germany. At the same time, the ethical–political distinction makes Habermas able to exclude fundamentalists. He writes that 'political integration does not extend to fundamentalist immigrant cultures. But neither does it justify compulsory assimilation for the sake of the self-affirmation of the cultural form of life dominant in the country' (ibid., 229). When talking about fundamentalism, Habermas is referring to groups and individuals that are not self-reflexive about their way of life. They do not accept that the pluralism of modern life puts limits on politics; that is, they do not accept the ethical–political distinction and the priority of the political over the ethical. Thus, fundamentalism consists in the attempt to impose – if necessary by force – one ethical conception of the good on society as a whole (ibid., 223f.; 2002, 150f.; 2006b, 9–11).[4]

Habermas's deliberative version of constitutional democracy is not neutral because it is linked to a conception of autonomy as rational self-legislation (Habermas 1996a, 445f.; 1996b, 1505). What is more the ethical–political distinction is not as sharp as one may first think. '*Ideally*', he writes, 'legal rules . . . regulate a matter in the equal interest of all those affected and to that extent give expression to generalizable interests' (Habermas 1996a, 154, emphasis added). However, Habermas (ibid., 155f.) also admits that legal norms are necessarily marked by some ethical particularity because, unlike moral norms, legal norms are positive and cannot be universal because they are linked to the democratic self-legislation of a particular demos. Although legal norms may rest on some consideration of what is equally good for all, they are also the expression of what we – here and now, in this polity – believe must be done. Thus, the political level cannot be completely abstract from a particular collective subject, even if the latter is only conceived as a demos and not as an ethnos.

Supposedly, each political order interprets the same set of universal and rationally reconstructable rights, the system of rights. But, in doing so, the interpretations are nonetheless tied to the particular demos:

> Legal orders as wholes are also 'ethically imbued' in that they interpret the universalistic content of the same constitutional principles in different ways, namely, against the background of the experiences that make up a national history and in light of a historically prevailing tradition, culture and form of life. (Habermas 1998b, 144)

Legal norms are split between a universal and a particular content. Habermas's solution is to insist that the political must nonetheless remain distinguished from the ethical, the demos from the ethnos. He writes that the particularity of the demos 'cannot detract from the legal system's neutrality vis-à-vis communities that are ethically integrated at a subpolitical level. . . . It is crucial to maintain the distinction between the two levels of integration' (ibid., 225). Thus, while the ethical–political distinction

> in no way forbids the citizens of a democratic constitutional state to assert a conception of the good in their general legal order, a conception they already share or have come to agree on through political discussion. It does, however, forbid them to privilege one form of life at the expense of others *within* the nation. (ibid., 220)

Even if society is integrated through common values, if these are political ones, then the hierarchical distinction between the ethical and the political can remain intact. Only then is it possible to include the other, to paraphrase Habermas (ibid.; critically Bernstein 1996).

(3) Habermas (1996a, 500; 1998b, 118, 225) concretizes these ideas with the notion of constitutional patriotism. A constitutional patriotism is, as the name suggests, a patriotism of the constitution, that is, of the constitutional principles and the way they have been institutionalized in political institutions and rights. Thus it should be distinguished from nationalism. Constitutional patriotism is a patriotism of the demos rather than the ethnos, and through it one can create a common 'we' while at the same time including different ethical conceptions of the good life. Habermas (1998b, 118) concludes:

> The political culture of a country crystallizes around its constitution. Each national culture develops a distinctive interpretation of those constitutional principles that are equally embodies in other republican constitutions – such as popular sovereignty and human rights – in light of its own national history. A 'constitutional patriotism' based on these interpretations can take the place originally occupied by nationalism.

Thus, constitutional patriotism is Janus faced: it has a universal content (the system of rights), but is a particular, contextual interpretation of that universal content, an interpretation that is relative to a particular political 'we'.

In conclusion, 'democratic citizenship need not be rooted in the national identity of a people. However, regardless of the diversity of different cultural forms of life, it does require that every citizen be socialized into a common political culture' (Habermas 1996a, 500; critically Michelman 1999). This view has implications for immigration policy, among other things. As mentioned above, Habermas (1998b, 226–36) believes that immigrants should not be required to assimilate into a national ethnos, they are only required to integrate at the political level. If immigration poses a threat to the national purity of the nation-state, then this is no threat to worry about, because what matters is that there exists a common political culture, and one should not confuse the political with the ethical, the demos with the ethnos.

Europe

Above I looked at Habermas's response to the first threat to the nation-state, the threat from within. That threat is mainly a threat to the *nation*-state, that is, to the nation-state as based on an ethnos. Habermas believes that this should lead us to a post-national approach; this is what is implied in the emphasis on the demos (as opposed to the ethnos), in the distinction between the ethical and the political and in the notion of constitutional patriotism. He is not saying that we should discard of the nation-state, only that the state must be post-national – that is, in a sense it should not be a *nation*-state, because it should not rest on ethical values, but only on political values.

In this and in the following section, I shall look at a second way in which Habermas believes that we should take a post-national approach. He believes that we must complement the nation-state with regional and global polities, even if the latter should not take the form of states properly speaking. Here the focus is on the state in nation-*state*, and this reflects the threats to the nation-state from without. Primarily those threats result from the increasing interdependence among societies and the dependence on the global market, both of which undermine the state's ability to make sovereign decisions. It is especially important in relation to the taxation that forms the basis for the welfare state (Habermas 2001b, 69–71; 2006b, 176f.).

In this section, I focus on Habermas's (1998b, chapter 6; 2001b, 89–103; 2006a, part IV; 2006b, part II; 2009, part II) idea that we must build regional polities, especially at the European level. This is, then, a question of the future of the European Union (EU). It is necessary to build a regional, European polity – so Habermas – as a counterweight to multinational companies and to the global markets. The EU should have a role to play in putting together economic and financial policies. In addition it should play a role in the spread of human rights and peace; it should help bring about an international legal order (Habermas 2006b, chapter 3). The EU should not, and cannot, develop into a state on the model of the nation-state, but the countries making up the EU ought to integrate their societies more and develop the EU institutions more in order that the EU becomes more capable of making decisions and realizing policies.

With regard to the institutions of a more integrated Europe, it is worth singling out one issue close to Habermas's heart, namely the development of a pan-European public sphere. Often we talk about a democratic deficit in the EU, and sometimes the EU Parliament is referred to as a Mickey Mouse parliament that has no real influence. Habermas agrees with these criticisms. For him, what is missing is that the EU institutions become rooted in a common European public sphere; that is, institutions, policies and decisions must become rooted in the opinion- and will-formation of the citizens of the EU. A common public sphere would complement the national public spheres, and it should be developed hand in hand with a common political culture. Habermas (1998b, 160) writes:

> [F]rom a normative perspective there can be no European federal state worthy of the title of a European democracy unless a European-wide, integrated public sphere develops in the ambit of a common political culture: a civil society encompassing interest associations, nongovernmental organizations, citizens' movements, etc., and naturally a party system appropriate to a European arena.

Only if policies are rooted in public deliberations on a Europe-wide scale will the citizens of the EU be able to see themselves not just as the subjects to those policies but also as their authors.

A common political culture must be just that: political, and not ethnic, religious, or ethical in any other way. The common political culture should not be the expression of a pre-political and given European identity, as if there existed an European ethnos with a common ethical identity. For instance, a shared political culture cannot be based on a (non-existing) shared religion. If there is a European people, it will be a people *qua* demos, not ethnos (ibid., 159). Habermas (ibid., 161; see also 2006b, 80f.) concludes that the identity of a European citizenry is something constructed through a political process:

> The ethical-political self-understanding of citizens in a democratic community must not be taken as a historical-cultural a priori that makes democratic will-formation possible, but rather as the fluid content of a circulatory process that is generated through a legal institutionalization of citizens' communication.

Thus, the common political culture is very much tied to the institution of the public sphere, and the two develop hand in hand.

To exemplify Habermas's views on Europe and the European Union, consider a newspaper article he published on 31 May 2003 in the wake of the US led invasion of Iraq. The piece – 'February 15, or: What Binds Europeans' – was written by Habermas, but co-signed by Jacques Derrida, and it was published simultaneously in German (in *Frankfurter Allgemeine Zeitung*) and French (in *Libération*) on the same day as pieces by other philosophers in other European newspapers (see Levy et al. 2005). The article refers to three dates, or events, that Habermas believes form part of an emerging European public sphere. There is, first, the date of the publication of the article together with the articles by other philosophers in other newspapers (31 May 2003). Second, there is 30 January 2003, when eight European heads of government published an open letter urging Europe to stand shoulder by shoulder with their American allies. And, third, there is 15 February 2003 which saw demonstrations across Europe and the rest of the world against the imminent Iraq war. In each case, there is an appeal to something like a trans-national, European public.

In the article, Habermas argues that Europe – meaning the EU – must play a greater role in the world, especially as a locomotive for the institutionalization of an international legal order and for the promotion of human rights and peace. In order for the EU to be able to play that role, a 'core Europe' – presumably consisting of Germany, France and the Benelux countries – must move ahead with integration, acting as a locomotive for further EU integration. (i.e. Habermas is advocating an EU at different speeds).

Apart from this more institutional proposal, what is also interesting is Habermas's argument that Europe may have a common identity based on shared historical experiences. Importantly, this should not, and cannot, be some natural, pre-political identity. Rather, it should be an identity articulated and constructed in response to a shared history. These historical experiences distinguish Europe from the rest of the world, including the United States (Habermas 2006b, 43–8). The historical experiences shared by Europeans are both negative (nationalism, totalitarianism and colonialism) and positive (the Enlightenment, the welfare state, secularism and the end to the use of violence as punishment, including the death penalty). The experiences form the basis for a common political identity, and it is easy to see whom this identity should be differentiated from, namely the US of George W. Bush (for criticisms, see Levy et al. 2005).

Cosmopolitan law

As with his proposal for a stronger EU, Habermas's proposal for more and stronger international law is in response to the threat to the nation-state from globalization (Habermas 1998b, 68ff.). And again the solution is not to either hang on to or discard the nation-state, but to build complementary structures and institutions, this time at the global level. If our lives depend on decisions taken beyond the nation-state, then democracy should be extended accordingly, being for the moment mainly tied to the nation-state. Again, this response is based on Habermas's conception of autonomy as the identity between addressees and authors of the laws: to be autonomous is to be able to see oneself as not just at the receiving end of decisions and policies but also as the ultimate source of those decisions and policies.

To understand Habermas's views on cosmopolitan law, it is useful to look at how he criticizes Kant's proposal for a cosmopolitan order (Kant 1991b; Habermas 1998b, chapter 7; 2006b, chapter 8). Here I shall only summarize Habermas's critique of Kant and not enter into any discussion of Kant or of Habermas's reading of Kant. In 'Perpetual Peace', Kant (1991b) proposes a 'perpetual peace', to be distinguished from a merely provisional peace which can always revert back into self-interest and war. But Kant does not reject (nation-)

state sovereignty or the so-called Westphalian order whereby states are sovereign and cannot intervene in the internal affairs of other states. The perpetual peace is to be brought about by a 'federation of nations' rather than a 'state of all peoples'. He now considers such a world state unfeasible, and, within the federation of states, the states are sovereign,[5] and so, although the peace is 'perpetual', it is not enforced by any supra-state entity and it depends on moral obligation.

While Habermas considers himself a Kantian and develops his own view of cosmopolitanism in dialogue with Kant, he is also critical of Kant. Habermas believes that we must not take (nation-)state sovereignty as a given. This is a problem in relation to Kant (1991b, 105) who approaches the issue of cosmopolitan law and government on the model of the move from a state of nature to the state of society. But this analogy is false, Habermas (2006b, 129f.) argues, and it tends to naturalize the only historical given nation-states; it assumes that the state is the natural entity for government and law. What is more, the move from states to a supra-state is complementary to the move from a state of nature to a state. This is so because citizens in (republican) states already enjoy the status of free and equal citizens (at least in theory). So the move to a cosmopolitan order is not meant to constitute subjects as citizens, that is, as legal subjects enjoying private and public autonomy. The move from states to a cosmopolitan order is only meant to complement the freedom citizens achieve by virtue of being citizens in republican states; in short, it is only meant to guarantee this freedom more fully and in response to the interdependence among states.

Cosmopolitan right ought, according to Habermas, to be legally instituted, that is, it must be right, not morality. Cosmopolitan right requires backing by force, although not necessarily backing by a world government: 'a world domestic policy . . . without a world government' (Habermas 2001b, 104). Habermas (1998b, 186–8; 2006b, 107–9, 135–9) proposes a 'multilevel' model of governance, which includes local, national, regional and global levels of governance. At the global level, a reformed United Nations would address issues such as human rights, war and peace, and risk. The United Nations – or any similar global institution – would not pursue economic and social policies, however. This would instead be the domain of regional institutions, such as the EU, at an intermediate level.

Given that cosmopolitan right should be legal and not (only) moral, this has implications for the form it can take. Here I shall mention two of these implications because they are important for Habermas.

First, cosmopolitan right cannot be truly universal because, as law, it is positive, and as such it is linked to a democratic subject (Habermas 2001b, 107–10). Even if this democratic subject is not a national or an ethical one, it will still not be a purely universal one. The law will be impregnated by political values (ibid., 108).

Second, cosmopolitan right must consist of legal and not merely moral norms. Morality is too weak to support the protection of peace and human rights; for this we need positive law, and hence there is a difference between Habermas and Kant here.[6] From Habermas's perspective, the result is that Carl Schmitt's critique of human rights is misguided. Schmitt confuses human rights with morality, whereas Habermas points out that human rights are *rights*, that is, positive legal norms. While we must be careful when spreading human rights across the world, and be sensitive to the cultural differences that characterize different states, we should not see human rights simply as ideological masks for the power of a particular nation or group of nations, as Schmitt does (Schmitt 1996, Habermas 1998b, 134–8, 193–201; see also 1989b, chapter 5; 1997, 107–17). Even if human rights are linked, via their positive nature, to a democratic will, they cannot be reduced to this. So, on the one hand, human rights are not reducible to morality and as such they cannot fulfil the ideological function of masking bestiality, as Schmitt would have it; and, on the other hand, human rights have a universal content and cannot be reduced to the will of any particular democratic subject. Human rights are Janus faced: at once particular and universal.

Habermas believes that a cosmopolitan order cannot be a world state, only a cosmopolitan law that protects peace and human rights. He believes this is within the realm of possibility, and his argument is both conceptual and empirical in this regard. Conceptually, if we take autonomy, conceived as rational self-legislation, seriously, then some form of supra-national law and government is necessary. This is so because those subject to decisions must be able to see themselves as also the authors of those decisions. In other words, the globalization of the economy, the environment and so on, necessitates a globalization of governance.

However, this does not tell us if a cosmopolitan order is possible. Here Habermas turns to a strategy also used by Kant in his time

(Habermas 2006b, 125f.). He finds signs in the present that point towards the possibility of a cosmopolitan order. The present post-national order meets the ideal of a cosmopolitan order halfway, and so the ideal is not utopian but connected to our present reality. The signs that Habermas (1998b, 171–8; 2006b, 143–6) single out are the following: the globalization of society (market, culture and so on), even if one should not overlook imperialism and inequality; the human rights discourse and institutions that have emerged since the end of World War II, even if human rights are instituted in an uneven and selective fashion; and the supra-national institutions such as the UN and the EU, even if these suffer from a democratic deficit. Thus Habermas is not blind to the imperfections of our present, post-national constellation, but for him the glass is half full rather than half empty because we can build on the progress already made.

I will end this section with an example of how Habermas thinks about the creation of a cosmopolitan order and the problems with this. The example is a newspaper article Habermas (2006a, chapter 2; see also 2006b, 29f., 85–7) wrote on the occasion of the NATO bombardments of Serbia and of Serbians in Kosovo in 1999. The essay is an example of how Habermas views the move 'from power politics to cosmopolitan society', to quote the title of the essay.

On the one hand, the international community did something to protect basic human rights in Kosovo. On the other hand, the international community was represented by NATO led by the United States, and they did not have the backing of the UN because of the opposition from Russia and China in the Security Council. This made the NATO bombardments problematic because they rested on the presumption that NATO represented the international community as well as the Kosovars on the ground: 'given the under-institutionalization of cosmopolitan law, such a politics is in many respects compelled to become a mere *anticipation* of the future cosmopolitan condition which it simultaneously seeks to realize' (Habermas 2006a, 27). And he continues:

> Even 19 undoubtedly democratic [NATO] states, as long as they authorize their own intervention, remain partisan. They are expressing a power of interpretation and decision-making which, if things were properly conducted, could only be exercised

by independent institutions. To this extent, they are acting paternalistically. (ibid., 29)

Habermas (ibid.) concludes that 'the incompleteness of the cosmopolitan condition demands exceptional sensitivity'. Habermas tentatively supported the war, although he later wrote more critically of the war and that there ought to be a halt to the bombardments (Habermas 1999).

Habermas's essay on the Kosovo War raises a number of important issues in relation to his defence of cosmopolitan right. First of all, the cosmopolitan order is not currently in place, but there are some signs in the present that such an order may be realizable in the future. This is so even if there are serious structural obstacles such as inequalities in power among states and in the make-up of the UN Security Council.

Second, the institutionalization and protection of human rights involves a risk of moralization. This is the risk that Schmitt pointed to. It arises from the moralization of one's own cause and, thereby, the bestialization of the enemy, who can then be bombed from the safe distance of the moral high ground. The original German title of Habermas's essay was tellingly 'Bestiality and Morality: A War on the Border between Law and Morality'. Habermas is aware of this danger that arises when violence is perpetrated in the name of a higher morality and without the more secure foundation of law that has been democratically mediated. One must, he argues, be sensitive to the voice of the other, especially when this voice is marginalized by structures of power in the contemporary world (see also Habermas 1998b, 146–50).

Third, and related to this, as is evident from the quotes from the essay, Habermas is weary of the paternalistic attitude of someone who 'anticipates' what a cosmopolitan order will entail at the very moment when that agent is also institutionalizing that order. This point should be seen in the context of the importance of autonomy. Such paternalism is criticizable precisely because it is opposed to autonomy. Yet, we must also ask how it is possible to create a society of autonomous citizens out of agents who are not already autonomous. That is, how can we put autonomy in place in a way that is not paternalistic? And how can we put in place a cosmopolitan society in a way that does not rest on power politics? This is precisely the questions that Habermas's essay on the Kosovo War throws up.

THE POST-SECULAR CONSTELLATION

The distinction between ethical and political integration is central to Habermas's writings on tolerance (2008, part IV; 2009, chapter 5) and religion (2002; 2003b, 101–15; 2008, parts II–III; Habermas and Ratzinger 2005; see also Shaw 1999). The context of these writings is the multiculturalism of contemporary Western societies, that is, the pluralism within any particular society of different ethni or cultures, religions and languages. Due to this pluralism, it is impossible to integrate society at the ethical level because imposing one particular ethical conception of the good life would inevitably lead to exclusion. As a result, society must be integrated at the political level; only in that way is the inclusion of the other in her otherness possible. What should be shared is a political culture crystallized around a constitutional patriotism. The ethical–political distinction makes possible 'a *nonlevelling* and *nonappropriating* inclusion of the other *in his otherness*' (Habermas 1998b, 40), because '[c]itizens who share a common political life also are others to one another, and each is entitled to *remain* an Other' (Habermas 2001b, 19). The questions that arise in the context of tolerance and religion are then: is tolerance the way to achieve this inclusion of the other? And, is there a place for religion in the public life of such a society?

Tolerance

It is often argued that tolerance is paradoxical. The paradox takes two forms. First, there is no tolerance without intolerance. 'There can be no inclusion without exclusion', Habermas (2008, 253) writes.

> The ostensible paradox is that every act of toleration must circumscribe the range of behavior that everybody must accept, thereby setting limits to tolerance itself. . . . And as long as this line is drawn in an authoritarian manner, i.e., unilaterally, the toleration bears the stigma of arbitrary exclusion.

Second, the relationship between the tolerating and the tolerated is asymmetrical. Habermas (2006b, 22) writes that

> [T]he act of toleration retains the connotation of a burden, an act of mercy or 'granting a favor'. One party allows the other a certain

amount of deviation from 'normality' on one condition: that the tolerated minority does not overstep the 'boundary of tolerance'.

Thus, on the face of it, tolerance is not the right way to include the other in her otherness and on an equal footing. This is so because, it would seem, tolerance merely reproduces the power of the strongest, for instance of the majority religion.

Habermas's solution to the two forms of the paradox of tolerance is to change the way we approach tolerance. It should come as no surprise that he believes that the paradoxes of tolerance – arbitrariness and asymmetry – can be dissolved if we think of tolerance in *intersubjectivist* terms. The problem with traditional conceptions of tolerance, Habermas argues, is that they rely on the philosophy of the subject. When it comes to the justification of tolerance, the justification is unilateral: somebody decides to tolerate (or not tolerate) somebody else. The decision and the justification for the decision to tolerate rest with a collective or individual subject. Habermas believes that the decision and justification must stand the test of intersubjective probing. They must be subject to deliberation among all those affected by the decision and by the norms of tolerance, and this includes those on the receiving end of tolerance. This is how Habermas (2003c, 5f.) puts it:

> [R]eciprocal religious toleration called for by everyone must rest on universally acceptable limits of tolerance. This consensual delimitation can arise only through the mode of deliberation in which those involved are obliged to engage in mutual perspective-taking. The legitimating power of such a deliberation is generalized and institutionalized only in the process of democratic will-formation.

Thus, Habermas believes that if conceived in intersubjectivist terms, the limit of tolerance can be rationalized as opposed to arbitrary, and the relationship between the tolerating and the tolerated can be one of reciprocity as opposed to asymmetry. In this way, tolerance can be a way to include the other in an unbiased fashion.

Religion

Habermas has developed his conception of tolerance in tandem with a conception of the role of religion in contemporary society. In this context, he talks about 'post-secularism'. For Habermas, religions are examples of ethical conceptions of the good life. This is so to the extent that, at times, he collapses the ethical–political distinction with the religious–secular distinction. Habermas thinks of the development of societies as a progression from pre-modern, religious societies over modern, secular societies to contemporary, post-secular societies. The development is thought of as a learning process.[7]

What is *post*-secular about post-secular societies is that they do not treat religion as something that will one day go away once we have become more rational. In this sense, the idea of 'post-secularism' is Habermas's response to the (new) importance of religion in the contemporary world. However, for Habermas, post-secularism also means that religions should be treated merely as ethical conceptions of the good among other ethical conceptions of the good. Religious differences should be tolerated as religious, or ethical, differences within a shared secular, or political, order. In other words, religion is here to stay, but only within otherwise secular societies. Habermas is not advocating that we overturn secularism.

The conditions under which religious differences are tolerated are revealing of the way Habermas conceives of tolerance and religion. Religious constituencies must be reflexive. By that Habermas means that they must accept that their validity claims – including their religious validity claims to what is a good life – are limited by three things: first, scientific knowledge; second, the secular state which must remain so; and, third, the pluralism of conceptions of the good life, including other religions. If they do not accept these conditions, the religious views and practices can be labelled 'fundamentalist' in the sense used above (Habermas 1998b, 223f.; 2002, 150f.; 2006b, 9–11).

There is a place for religious reasons in the public, but, before they can become politically effective, they must be translated into political reasons. Habermas (2008, 130) refers to an 'institutional translation proviso' in this regard. His point is that religious reasons must be translated into political ditto if they are to count as reasons for others than the believers of the religion in question. The language of religious reasons is not excluded from the public sphere, but persons running for, or holding, public office must refrain from using religious reasons (Habermas 2008, 128f.). In order to count within the political system, religious reasons must first be translated into 'a language, that is equally accessible to all citizens' – that is, a 'political' language (ibid., 122). The political language is a shared, 'public' language that everybody can share irrespective of whether they have been initiated into a particular religion or have had religious truth revealed to them.

Religious and non-religious individuals and groups are on a par in a post-secular society. It is a society that does not maintain that religions are irrational and backward (*post*-secular), but does insist that the common ground between religious and non-religious constituencies must be secular (post-*secular*). This is why the ethical–political and religious–secular distinctions are so important to Habermas. The political is the common ground of political institutions and a political culture within which we can have deliberations that are not biased from the outset against any particular ethical conception of the good life. The deliberations include deliberations about the right norms of (religious) tolerance.

The equal inclusion of different ethical views and practices comes with a caveat though. The caveat is that the deliberations cannot be neutral vis-à-vis the 'fundamentalist', and so the 'fundamentalist' is excluded from seeing his views transformed into public policy. As described above, the fundamentalists are those who insist on imposing their ethical worldviews – for instance, religions – on others through the state and the law, and this is what the ethical–political distinction guards against.

Habermas may be criticized from two opposing sides. First it may be asked why we rational and atheist citizens should take religious beliefs and reasons seriously. If we believe that religious beliefs are not just wrong but also irrational, and if religious reasons can never be reasons for us because they are based on religious revelation, then there seems no reason why we should take them seriously. On this view, Habermas's idea of post-secularism is a step in the wrong direction, reflecting the prominent, but unfortunate, place of religion in today's world. On this view, then, the response should not be post-secularism, but to insist even more on secularism.

From the opposite perspective, the following question arises: even if Habermas seeks to take religion and religious reasons seriously, is his solution not biased against religion from the very beginning? Habermas may speak of a post-secular society, and he may ask non-believers to listen to religious reasons, but ultimately religion is forced to play the secularist game. This is so because, although there is a place for religion in the post-secular society, it is only in civil society and the public sphere and not within the political system or in the law.

In short, when things get serious, religious reasons must be translated into political ditto. Religion is tolerable as long as it has no political power. In their exchange, Habermas and Joseph Ratzinger (the later Pope Benedictus XVI) seem to agree that reason and religion need and can learn from one another (Habermas and Ratzinger 2005). However, for Habermas, the relationship is not a symmetrical one because, when it comes to democracy and law, religious reason must yield to the public use of reason that Habermas has reconstructed in his theories of communicative reason, discourse ethics and deliberative democracy.

THE NEW CONSTELLATION OF HUMAN NATURE

In this final section, I will present Habermas's writings on new gene technologies (cloning, embryonic stem cell research, and so on) from around the turn of the century (Habermas 2001b, chapter 8; 2003b; see also Mendieta 2002). Gene technology is another one of those new issues that may change the way we think about politics, morality and the world. Together with globalization, multiculturalism and the resurgence of religion, the new gene technologies create a new political constellation. It should come as no big surprise that Habermas (2003b, 22) looks at this issue through the lens of discourse ethics and constitutional democracy. For him, it is a matter of the justifiability of gene technological interventions, and justifiability is, in turn, a matter of public justifiability as stipulated in the theories of discourse ethics and deliberative democracy.

The problem with using gene technology on foetuses is, for Habermas, essentially a problem of paternalism. What is problematic about this sort of gene technology is that it involves judging whether other persons' lives are worth living (ibid., 69). That judgement can only be asymmetrical and one-sided – that is, paternalistic – and this of course goes against the principle of autonomy. Habermas (ibid., 14; see also 65) writes that 'when a person makes an irreversible decision about the natural traits of another person, . . . the fundamental symmetry of responsibility that exists among free and equal persons is restricted'. When used in this way, gene technology introduces an asymmetry between the ones carrying out the genetic intervention (for instance, the doctors and the parents) and the one subjected to the intervention. The latter is taken as an object and becomes instrumentalized life: life as a means to someone else's end rather than life as an end in itself, thus 'obliterating the boundary between persons and things' (ibid., 13; see also 49).

As opposed to this, autonomy is only possible on the background of an idea of human dignity where each person is taken as irreplaceable and singular. One must treat other persons as deserving of respect irrespective of what they are 'for us'. Importantly, Habermas understands autonomy in terms of communicative rationality, and the other person should therefore be seen as a potential partner in a symmetrical and inclusive dialogue:

> [I]n the case of therapeutic gene manipulations, we approach the embryo as the second person he will one day be. This clinical attitude draws its legitimizing force from the well-founded counterfactual assumption of a possible consensus reached with another person who is capable of saying yes or no. The burden of normative proof is thus shifted to the justification of an anticipated consent that at present cannot be sought. (ibid., 43, emphasis removed)

We must treat the gene manipulated embryo as a potential partner in a dialogue to decide the justifiability of the intervention.

Importantly, 'the potential harm lies not at the level of a deprivation of the rights of a legal person, but rather in the uncertain status of a person as a bearer of potential rights' (ibid., 78). Thus, for Habermas the embryo is not (yet) a legal person or a bearer of rights. This does not in itself justify manipulation of it because we must ask what must be the case so that one day the embryo may develop into a person who can be the bearer of rights. That is, we must ask what must be the case in order that the embryo may one day become an autonomous and moral person. Habermas's answer to that question is that the person should not be able to see itself as the result of somebody else's manipulation of her nature.

To be a person is to be taken by others as a voice deserving of equal respect (ibid., 34f.). However, this means, among other things, that the person must be herself and must, literally and metaphorically, be at home in her own body, and here bodily and personal integrity converge (ibid., 57). Without autonomy in this respect too, the person will not be able to be an equal partner in dialogue.

It is on the basis of this notion of autonomy that Habermas engages with gene technology and human nature. He distinguishes between two kinds of gene technological interventions (ibid., 51f.). First there are clinical, therapeutic interventions aimed at healing disease; it includes such things as strengthening the immune system or prolonging life (ibid., 51). These are for the good of the patient taken as a full person, and they assume the potential future consent of the patient. That is, with these interventions we can assume that the patient can, at a later stage, engage in communicative relations on an equal footing with the doctor or parent. Habermas is positive towards this use of gene technology. Although the distinction is difficult to uphold (ibid.),[8] clinical interventions can be distinguished from manipulative, or enhancing, interventions. Here the aim is to create 'better' human beings, according to a standard laid down by those making the interventions (the doctor, the parents or society). For instance, it could be interventions to create human beings with, or without, a particular hair colour. Here the (future) person is taken as an object to be instrumentalized, and Habermas (ibid., 52, 62) is critical of this use of gene technology.

Habermas's writings on gene technology and human nature are not only, or even primarily, interesting for his position on these issues, but also for the way he believes these issues can be settled. Here two things are important.

Primarily, as we have seen, any intervention – whether clinical or manipulative – must be justified and it must be so in a dialogue that includes the person on whom the intervention is carried out, even if this can only be done in an attitude of anticipation. (And here one should not forget Habermas's warnings about the thin line between this anticipatory attitude and paternalism in the case of Kosovo, cf. above pp. 151f.) Thus, we must treat the embryo as a potential future partner in dialogue, even if this does not give the embryo any legal rights, and so this is not an argument against abortion. This much also follows from Habermas's notion of autonomy.

Secondly, any justification must take place within the limits of constitutional democracy. The issue of gene technology and human nature should be treated as a moral question, and any political and legal regulation of it should not be based on any particular ethical worldview but only on political reasons potentially available to everybody (ibid., 32f.). Thus, although religious reasons are allowed a place

in public deliberations about gene technology, we cannot base legislation on any particular religious views of human nature.

CONCLUSION

In this chapter, I have presented Habermas's views on three issues
in contemporary society: the post-national constellation, the post-
secular constellation and the new constellation of human nature.
In each new constellation of politics, our traditional conceptions of
politics and society are challenged – by globalization, by multiculturalism and the resurgence of religion and by new gene technologies,
respectively. Each case also challenges Habermas's theories of discourse ethics and deliberative democracy.

Habermas's response to the three new constellations is a version of
the public use of reason: to insist on the separation between ethnos
and demos and that the latter's public will-formation should be the
basis for laws; the importance of a supra-national (European, global)
public sphere; the equality of ethical conceptions of the good life,
including religions, and the separation of the ethical and the political; and the autonomy of persons capable of giving reasons and justifying their positions in public and to one another.

In these ways, Habermas's treatment of the issues covered in this
chapter again highlights what is the red thread running through
his work, namely the public use of reason. An early version of this is
announced in *The Structural Transformation of the Public Sphere*
(1989a). In the appendix to *Knowledge and Human Interests*, Habermas
(1987b, 314) starts to spell out this idea in a more systematic form
when he insists that '[w]hat raises us out of nature is the only thing
whose nature we can know: language. Through its structure, autonomy and responsibility are posited for us'. This is then spelled out
in *The Theory of Communicative Action* (1984; 1987a), 'Discourse
Ethics' (in 1990) and *Between Facts and Norms* (1996a). In a more
recent interview, Habermas (1994, 97) insists that this idea of
the force of public argumentation is present in his work in the form
of democracy:

> If there is any small remnant of utopia that I've preserved, then it
> is surely the idea that democracy – and the public struggle for its
> best form – is capable of hacking through the Gordian knots of
> otherwise insoluble problems. I'm not saying that we're going to

succeed in this; we don't even know whether success is possible. But because we don't know, we at least have to try.

Habermas's interventions in debates about the nation-state, Europe and cosmopolitan law, about tolerance and religion, and about gene technology also highlight his long-standing engagement in public debates as a public intellectual. His philosophical writings and his occasional pieces in newspapers reflect one another, and his political positions are clearly influenced by his philosophy, and vice versa. Despite this symbiotic relationship between theory and practice, and between philosophy and politics, it is worth ending with a sobering note of caution, hit by someone who has spent his life theorizing:

Young people today expect something more from philosophy, and they're naturally disappointed when their studies don't teach them how to solve the problems of their own lives – in Frankfurt, at any rate, nobody claims to be able to tell them. [. . .] In any case, it's good not to expect any more or anything different from theories than what they can achieve – and that's little enough. (ibid., 99f.; see also 2003a, chapter 7)

FURTHER READINGS

For Habermas's writings on the nation-state, Europe and cosmopolitanism, see the essays and interviews in *The Past as Future* (1994), *A Berlin Republic* (1997), parts II–IV of *The Inclusion of the Other* (1998b), *The Postnational Constellation* (2001b), *Time of Transitions* (2006a), *The Divided West* (2006b) and *Europe* (2009) as well as Appendix II to *Between Facts and Norms* (1996a). For critical appraisals, see Müller (2000) and Levy et al. (2005). For Habermas on religion and tolerance, see the essays in *Religion and Rationality* (2002) and in parts II–IV of *Between Naturalism and Religion* (2008). For Habermas's writings on cloning, see *The Future of Human Nature* (2003b) and *The Postnational Constellation* (2001b, chapter 8) as well as Mendieta (2002).

NOTES

1 There are two notable exceptions to this: first, Matuštík's (2001) introduction to Habermas and his social, cultural and political context; and, second, a recent autobiographical essay by Habermas (2008, chapter 1).

CHAPTER 1   TOWARDS A CRITICAL THEORY OF SOCIETY

1 See the website of the Institute for Social Research: http://www.ifs. uni-frankfurt.de/english/index.htm.
2 Note that here, in his earlier work and like Habermas, Horkheimer does not reject rationalization as such, whereas in his later work, including *Dialectic of Enlightenment*, he tends to do so.
3 The history of Marxism provides a good example of this conundrum: can the proletariat achieve its own emancipation, or do they need a little help from its friends in the Party? If the proletariat is destined to be the agents of historical change, can we then just lean back and wait for it to happen by itself?
4 On Habermas and power, see, for instance, Honneth 1991 and Shabani 2003, especially chapter 6.
5 Habermas often focuses on practices of argumentation. Argumentation is just one form of communication among others, but he believes it is easier to discern the transcendental presuppositions of all communication in practices of argumentation. See also Chapters 3 and 4.

CHAPTER 2   THE PUBLIC SPHERE

1 On the history of the book and the translation, see Habermas 1992, 421f.
2 'By the first decade of the eighteenth century London already had 3,000 [coffeehouses], each with a core group of regulars.' Habermas 1989a, 32.
3 The classical statement of this argument is Pateman 1988, but see also Young 1986. For critiques of Habermas's *The Structural Transformation of the Public Sphere* along these lines, see Landes 1992, Eley 1992 and Fraser 1992.
4 For Habermas's response to this, see Habermas 1992a, 443f.
5 For the critique that Habermas overlooks the importance of the plebeian public sphere, see Negt and Kluge 1993, chapter 2 and 'Commentaries'.

6 All translations in the following are mine. Habermas's writings on the student movement are collected in parts I and II of Habermas 1981, and some essays have been translated in Habermas 1971, chapters 1–3. On Habermas and the student movement, see also Holub 1991, chapter 4.

7 In Chapter 5, I shall bring up another example of this, namely civil disobedience.

8 On this critique, see Holub 1991, 83f., 94–8. As Slavoj Žižek (2000, 326) has recently noted with reference to Habermas, 'the Left has a choice today: either it accepts the predominant liberal democratic horizon . . ., and engages in a hegemonic battle *within* it, *or it risks the opposite gesture of refusing its very terms, of flatly rejecting today's liberal blackmail that courting any prospect of radical change paves the way for totalitarianism.* It is my firm conviction, my politico-existential premises, that the old '68 motto *Soyons réalists, demandons l'impossible!* still holds . . . if this radical choice is decried by some bleeding-heart liberals as *Linksfascismus* [leftist Fascism], so be it!' The critique of Habermas is that sticking to the ideals of the bourgeois, liberal public sphere prevents him from seeing the potential for radical change from other quarters of society.

CHAPTER 3   COMMUNICATIVE ACTION AND REASON

1 For one of Habermas's clearest formulations of this, see Habermas 1987c, chapter 11 ('An Alternative Way out of the Philosophy of the Subject: Communicative versus Subject-Centered Reason').

2 Habermas develops his formal pragmatics in a number of places, but most importantly in Habermas 1998, 21–103. For a good brief introduction to Habermas's formal pragmatics and its relation to communicative action and reason, see Cooke 1998.

3 There are, in fact, four validity claims with intelligibility being the fourth. That is, when speaking, we also make an implicit claim that what we say is intelligible to a normal competent hearer.

4 Habermas (1987a, 121–3) uses the example of a building site, where a young worker is asked by his seniors to go fetch beer for the morning break.

5 On the first three, see Habermas 1984, 85–94; on the communicative model of action, see Habermas 1984, 94–101.

6 In his earlier work, Habermas (for instance, 2001a, 102f.) referred to rational discourse with the term 'ideal speech situation', a term he later discarded because it suggests an ideal to be approximated, when in reality it is a counterfactual assumption one makes when entering discourse (Habermas 1982, 261f.; 1993, 163f.).

7 For Habermas's reconstruction of these historical evolutionary processes, see Habermas 1987a, 156–97.

8 Habermas 1984, 288: 'the use of language with an orientation to reaching understanding is the *original mode* of language use, upon which . . . the instrumental use of language in general [is] parasitic'.

9 For different Critical Theory views of these conflicts, see the important debate between Nancy Fraser and Axel Honneth (2003) on redistribution

vs. recognition as the basic way of understanding contemporary social struggles. See also Honneth 1991.

10 See also Habermas's comments in Horster and van Reijen 1992. On new social movements and civil society from a perspective inspired by Habermas, see Cohen and Arato 1992.

11 See the essays in Kelly 1994. On Habermas and power more generally and from an alternative Critical Theory perspective, see Honneth 1991.

CHAPTER 4 DISCOURSE ETHICS

1 Earlier Habermas used the expression 'ideal speech situation', but he later discarded that expression because it might mistakenly suggest that it is a form of life that could be realized. For his use of 'the ideal speech situation', see Habermas 2001a, 102f. For the retraction of the term, see Habermas 1982, 261f.; 1993, 163f.

2 Initially Habermas conceived of this distinction as a distinction between different kinds of discourses, but he now conceives of it as different kinds of questions that can be raised with respect to the same matter and in the same discursive setting. Habermas 1996a, 159–68 and 565 (note 3).

3 Habermas (1992b, chapter 5; 1993, 52f.) has also drawn on the work of another influential American pragmatist, Charles Sanders Pierce (1839–1914).

4 See the different formulations in Habermas 2001a, 102f.; 1993, 145, 164.

5 For a well-developed Hegel inspired critique of Habermas from someone who is otherwise sympathetic to his project, see Benhabib 1986a.

6 Note two things though. First, for Habermas, the norms must have been discursively vindicated and the Kantian monological discourse is insufficient in this regard; but, second, it is not unreasonable to think that a Habermasian style discourse would come up with something like these norms.

7 For Habermas on these debates, see Habermas 1990, 195–215; 1993, chapters 1–3; and 1998b, chapters 8–9.

CHAPTER 5 DELIBERATIVE DEMOCRACY

1 For the argument that we cannot act only instrumentally or strategically in the long run, see Chapter 3. Recall also that, according to Habermas, strategic action ultimately relies on communicative action, because without the mutual understanding generated through communicative action, strategic actors would not be able to manipulate other agents.

2 The debate between Habermas and Rawls is very illuminating of both theorists' works. See Habermas 1996a, 56–65; 1998, chapters 2–3; Rawls 1995; Baynes 1992; McCarthy 1994.

3 For the view that Habermas has become more conservative and less critical from *Between Facts and Norms* onwards, see Shabani 2003; and Scheuerman 1999.

4 The same point is made by Habermas (1996a, xlii) in the quote from the Introduction: 'In the final analysis, private legal subjects cannot come to

enjoy equal individual liberties if they do not *themselves*, in the common exercise of their political autonomy, achieve clarity about justified interests and standards.' (See pp. 2–4 above.)

5 For criticisms of Habermas's attempt to reconcile constitutionalism and democracy, individual rights and popular sovereignty, see Cronin 2006, Ferrara 2001 and Honig 2006.

6 See also Cohen and Arato 1992, chapter 11 on Habermas's view of civil disobedience. For a critique and a defence of Habermas, see Thomassen 2007, chapter 4 and Smith 2008, respectively.

7 The issue is related to the distinction between justice and legitimacy, where, roughly speaking, legitimacy is dependent on the right procedures being followed and justice is independent of the procedures. Liberals typically accuse republicans and deliberative democrats of sacrificing justice to legitimacy. Simplifying, we may say that Habermas believes that justice and legitimacy converge insofar as we have constitutionalism *and* democracy, individual liberty rights and popular sovereignty.

8 It should be noted though that the decision has since been reversed. Most decisions will be partly reversible and partly irreversible.

9 For a critique of Habermas on this point from a post-structuralist perspective, see Honig 2006. On the republican critique of Habermas on this point, see Cronin 2006.

CHAPTER 6   THE NEW POLITICAL CONSTELLATION

1 The same issues resurfaced in debates about Germany's role during the first Gulf War and in the war in Kosovo. See Habermas 1994, 24–31 and 2006a, 19–21, respectively. I return to Habermas's views on the Kosovo War below. In the late 1990s, the debate about the normalization of the German past reappeared in the context of Daniel Goldhagen's book, *Hitler's Willing Executioners* (Habermas 2001b, chapter 2). The debate concerned, first, the critical self-reflection of present and future generations on their nation's past, and, second, how mass killings could become a 'normal' occurrence, perpetrated by 'normal' citizens. A similar debate took place in the late 1990s about the creation of a memorial in Berlin for the victims of the Holocaust (Habermas 2006a, chapter 4).

2 See Habermas's (2001b, chapter 1) account of the way German language and culture were created in the nineteenth century and contributed to the building of a German nation.

3 In a different place, Habermas (1997, 96) writes that with the form the reunification was taking, 'those who were eager to join can now only conform or submit: in any case there is no room for political action'. This lack of political action – of democratic mediation of the reunification – is precisely the problem Habermas had with the way reunification took place.

4 Habermas's (1998b, 118) position is clear from the following quote:

The level of the shared political culture must be uncoupled from the level of subcultures and their prepolitical identities. Of course, the claim to coexist with equal rights is subject to the proviso that the protected faiths and practices must not contradict the reigning constitutional principles (as they are interpreted by the political culture.

The ethical and the political must be distinguished; the political enjoys primacy over the ethical; and subcultures must accept the ethical–political distinction and the primacy of the political – if not, they are 'fundamentalist'.

5 Kant (1991b, 102; see also 105) writes that

> [A] *federation of peoples* . . . would not be the same thing as an international state. For the idea of an international state is contradictory, since every state involves a relationship between a superior (the legislator) and an inferior (the people obeying the laws), whereas a number of nations forming one state would constitute a single nation. And this contradicts our initial assumption, as we are here considering the right of nations in relation to one another insofar as they are a group of separate states which are not to be welded together as a unit.

6 The point is similar to the point Habermas makes about the need for law as a medium of societal integration in modern complex societies because morality is insufficient for this purpose. See Chapter 5 above.

7 This view of the history of societies ties in with Habermas's account of modernity and, in that context, the linguistification of the sacred as well as the developmental psychology of Piaget and Kohlberg, cf. above in Chapter 3. See also Adams 2006.

8 For instance, on which side of the distinction would a cleft palate, or 'hare lip', fall? Whether an intervention to reduce the risk of cleft palate would be 'clinical' or 'enhancing' would depend on, among other things, our conception of what exactly it means to be a full person capable of partaking in social life.

BIBLIOGRAPHY

Readers interested in literature on specific parts of Habermas's work should consult the 'Further Readings' sections at the end of each chapter. Years in square brackets refer to the original year of publication.

INTRODUCTIONS

Among the more advanced introductions to Jürgen Habermas's work, the best are the following. For introductions to Habermas's early, philosophical and critical work, two books are particularly useful: *Metacritique* by Garbis Kortian (1980) and *The Idea of Critical Theory: Habermas and the Frankfurt School* by Raymond Geuss (1981) (see the full references in the list of cited works below). Thomas McCarthy's (1978) *The Critical Theory of Jürgen Habermas* is an excellent introduction to Habermas's early work prior to the publication of *The Theory of Communicative Action*. *Habermas and the Dialectic of Reason* by David Ingram (1987) gives a thorough introduction to the theory of communicative action and rationality. Pieter Duvenage's (2003) *Habermas and Aesthetics* is a good introduction to Habermas's (limited) work on aesthetics and reconstructs the advantages and limitations of Habermas's communicative approach for aesthetics. In *Jürgen Habermas: Critic in the Public Sphere*, Robert Holub (1991) introduces Habermas as a public intellectual from the 1960s to the 1980s, and the book is useful for those who want to approach Habermas through his theoretical and political debates with other thinkers. Finally, in *Jürgen Habermas: A Philosophical–Political Profile*, Martin Matuštík (2001) places Habermas's philosophy and politics in the context of German culture and society.

HABERMAS ON HABERMAS

A useful road into Habermas's work goes via interviews with Habermas. In interviews, Habermas often presents his thoughts in a more accessible fashion, and often the interviews are given with laypersons in mind. The best collections of interviews with Habermas are *Autonomy and Solidarity*, edited by Peter Dews (1992), and *The Past as Future* (1994) with interviews on political topics.

Habermas's political writings are also usually a good way to approach his thinking because they situate his theoretical points in relation to concrete issues, and because they are often written for newspapers. Habermas has published 11 volumes of what he calls *Kleine Politische Schriften*, literally 'small political writings'. Many of these have been translated, and other more recent writings can be found on the internet. The most recent translation of political writings is *Europe* (2009).

Apart from his major statements of his philosophical and theoretical positions, Habermas often publishes short expositions of the major works. These provide good introductions to the longer and more difficult works. Where relevant, I have made references to these in the 'Further Readings' sections after each chapter.

The best short collection of Habermas's writings is William Outhwaite's *The Habermas Reader* (1996).

CRITICS

There are a number of edited volumes with discussions of Habermas and different aspects of his work. The best of them are the following: *Habermas: Critical Debates*, edited by John B. Thompson and David Held (1982) contains discussions of Habermas as a critical theorist, and Richard Bernstein's (1985) *Habermas and Modernity* contains good discussions of Habermas's thoughts on modernity and critical theory. For discussions of the theory of communicative action and rationality, see the contributions in *Communicative Action,* edited by Axel Honneth and Hans Joas (1991), and *Philosophical Investigations in the Unfinished Project of Enlightenment*, edited by Axel Honneth et al. (1992). *Habermas and the Unfinished Project of Modernity*, edited by Seyla Benhabib and Maurizio Passerin d'Entrèves (1997) has essays on Habermas's *The Philosophical Discourse of Modernity*. The best volume for critical discussions of Habermas's political philosophy is Michel Rosenfeld and Andrew Arato's (1998) *Habermas on Law and Democracy*. The best volumes with discussions of Habermas's work as a whole are Stephen White's (1995) *The Cambridge Companion to Habermas* and David Rasmussen and James Swindal's four volume *Jürgen Habermas* (2002a–d). See also the special issue of *New German Critique* (1985) devoted to Habermas's work.

Critique and Power, edited by Michael Kelly (1994) and *The Derrida–Habermas Reader*, edited by Lasse Thomassen (2006), set up encounters between Habermas and two of his post-structuralist opponents, Michel Foucault and Jacques Derrida, respectively.

FURTHER LITERATURE

The best online bibliography of Habermas's works can be found at http://www.habermasforum.dk/index.php?type=bibliografi2

CITED WORKS

Years in brackets refer to the first publication of the text.

Adams, N. (2006), *Habermas and Theology*. Cambridge: Cambridge University Press.

Austin, J. L. (1975) [1962], *How to Do Things with Words* (2nd edn). Oxford: Oxford University Press.

Baynes, K. (1992), *The Normative Grounds of Social Criticism: Kant, Rawls and Habermas*. Albany: State University of New York Press.

Benhabib, S. (1986a), *Critique, Norm, and Utopia: A Study of the Foundations of Critical Theory*. New York: Columbia University Press.

—(1986b), 'The Generalized and the Concrete Other: The Kohlberg-Gilligan Controversy and Feminist Theory', *Praxis International*, 5, (no. 4), 402–24. Also in S. Benhabib (1992), *Situating the Self: Gender, Community and Postmodernism in Contemporary Ethics*. London: Routledge, chapter 5.

—(1992), 'Models of Public Space: Hannah Arendt, the Liberal Tradition and Jürgen Habermas', in C. Calhoun (ed.), *Habermas and the Public Sphere*. Cambridge, MA: MIT Press, pp. 73–98.

Benhabib, S. and Dallmayr, F. (1990), *The Communicative Ethics Controversy*. Cambridge, MA: MIT Press.

Bernstein, J. M. (1995), *Recovering Ethical Life: Jürgen Habermas and the Future of Critical Theory*. London: Routledge.

Bernstein, R. J. (1996), 'The Retrieval of the Democratic Ethos', *Cardozo Law Review*, 17, (nos. 4–5), 1127–46. Reprinted in M. Rosenfeld and A. Arato (eds), *Habermas on Law and Democracy: Critical Exchanges*. Berkeley: University of California Press, 1996, pp. 287–306.

—(ed.) (1985), *Habermas and Modernity*. Cambridge, MA: MIT Press.

Bohman, J. (2000), *Public Deliberation: Pluralism, Complexity, and Democracy*. Cambridge, MA: MIT Press.

Bohman, J. and Rehg, W. (1997), *Deliberative Democracy: Essays on Reason and Politics*. Cambridge, MA: MIT Press.

Bottomore, T. (2002), *The Frankfurt School and Its Critics*. London: Routledge.

Calhoun, C. (ed.) (1992a), *Habermas and the Public Sphere*. Cambridge, MA: MIT Press.

—(1992b), 'Introduction: Habermas and the Public Sphere', in C. Calhoun (ed.), *Habermas and the Public Sphere*. Cambridge, MA: MIT Press, pp. 1–49.

Chambers, S. (1996), *Reasonable Democracy: Jürgen Habermas and the Politics of Discourse*. Ithaca: Cornell University Press.

Cohen, J. and Arato, A. (1992), *Civil Society and Political Theory*. Cambridge, MA: MIT Press.

Cooke, M. (1998), 'Introduction', in J. Habermas, *On the Pragmatics of Communication*, ed. and trans. M. Cooke. Cambridge: Polity Press, pp. 1–19.

Cronin, C. (2006), 'On the Possibility of a Democratic Constitutional Founding: Habermas and Michelman in Dialogue', *Ratio Juris*, 19, (no. 3), 343–69.

Culler, J. (1985), 'Communicative Competence and Normative Force', *New German Critique*, 35 (Spring/Summer), 133–44.

Deflem, M. (ed.) (1996), *Habermas, Modernity and Law*. London: Sage. Previously published as *Philosophy & Social Criticism*, 20, (no. 4), 1994.

Derrida, J. (1988), *Limited Inc*, trans. J. Mehlman and S. Weber. Evanston: Northwestern University Press.

Dews, P. (1992), *Autonomy and Solidarity: Interviews with Jürgen Habermas* (revised edn). London: Routledge.

Dryzek, J. (2000), *Deliberative Democracy and Beyond: Liberals, Critics, Contestations*. Oxford: Oxford University Press.

Duvenage, P. (2003), *Habermas and Aesthetics: The Limits of Communicative Reason*. Cambridge: Polity.

Eley, G. (1992), 'Nations, Publics, and Political Cultures: Placing Habermas in the Nineteenth Century', in C. Calhoun (ed.), *Habermas and the Public Sphere*. Cambridge, MA: MIT Press, pp. 289–339.

d'Entrèves , M. P. and Benhabib, S. (eds) (1997), *Habermas and the Unfinished Project of Modernity: Critical Essays on* The Philosophical Discourse of Modernity. Cambridge, MA: MIT Press.

Ferrara, A. (2001), 'Of Boats and Principles: Reflections on Habermas's "Constitutional Democracy"', *Political Theory*, 29, (no. 6), 782–9.

Finlayson, G. (1999), 'Does Hegel's Critique of Kant's Moral Theory Apply to Discourse Ethics?', in P. Dews (ed.), *Habermas: A Critical Reader*. Oxford: Blackwell, pp. 29–52.

Fraser, N. (1992), 'Rethinking the Public Sphere: A Contribution to the Critique of Actually Existing Democracy', in C. Calhoun (ed.), *Habermas and the Public Sphere*. Cambridge, MA: MIT Press, pp. 109–142. Reprinted in N. Fraser (1997), *Justice Interruptus: Critical Reflections on the "Postsocialist" Condition*. London: Routledge, chapter 3.

Fraser, N. (1997), *Justice Interruptus: Critical Reflections on the 'Postsocialist' Condition*. London: Routledge.

Fraser, N. and Honneth, A. (2003), *Redistribution or Recognition? A Political-Philosophical Exchange.* London: Verso.

Geuss, R. (1981), *The Idea of Critical Theory: Habermas & the Frankfurt School.* Cambridge: Cambridge University Press.

Gilligan, C. (1982), *In a Different Voice: Psychological Theory and Women's Development.* Cambridge, MA: Harvard University Press.

Gould, C. C. (1996), 'Diversity and Democracy: Representing Differences', in S. Benhabib (ed.), *Democracy and Difference: Contesting the Boundaries of the Political.* Princeton: Princeton University Press, pp. 171–86.

Günther, K. (1993) [1988], *The Sense of Appropriateness: Application Discourses in Morality and Law*, trans. J. Farrell. Albany: State University of New York.

Habermas, J. (1971) [1968/1969], *Toward a Rational Society: Student Protest, Science, and Politics*, trans. J. J. Shapiro. Boston: Beacon Press.

—(1980) [1970], 'The Hermeneutic Claim to Universality', in J. Bleicher (ed.), *Contemporary Hermeneutics: Hermeneutics as Method, Philosophy, and Critique.* London: Routledge, pp. 181–211.

—(1981), *Kleine Politische Schriften I–IV.* Frankfurt am Main: Suhrkamp.

—(1982), 'A Reply to My Critics', in J. B. Thompson and D. Held (eds), *Habermas: Critical Debates.* Cambridge, MA: MIT Press, pp. 219–83.

—(1983) [1980], 'Interpretive Social Science vs. Hermeneuticism', in N. Haan, R. N. Bellah, P. Rabinow and W. M. Sullivan (eds), *Social Science as Moral Inquiry.* New York: Columbia University Press, 1983, pp. 251–69.

—(1984) [1981], *The Theory of Communicative Action: Reason and the Rationalization of Society.* Vol. I, trans. T. McCarthy. Cambridge: Polity Press.

—(1985) [1983], 'Civil Disobedience: Litmus Test for the Democratic Constitutional State', trans. J. Torpey, *Berkeley Journal of Sociology*, 30, 95–116.

—(1987a) [1981], *The Theory of Communicative Action: The Critique of Functionalist Reason.* Vol. II, trans. T. McCarthy. Cambridge: Polity Press.

—(1987b) [1968], *Knowledge and Human Interests*, trans. J. J. Shapiro. Cambridge: Polity Press.

—(1987c) [1985], *The Philosophical Discourse of Modernity: Twelve Lectures*, trans. F. G. Lawrence. Cambridge: Polity Press.

—(1988a) [1963], *Theory and Practice*, trans. J. Viertel. Boston: Beacon Press.

—(1988b), 'Law and Morality', trans. K. Baynes, in S. M. McMurrin (ed.), *The Tanner Lectures on Human Values.* Vol. 8. Salt Lake City: University of Utah Press, pp. 217–79.

—(1988c) [1967], *On the Logic of Social Sciences*, trans. S. Weber Nicholson and J. A. Stark. Cambridge, MA: MIT Press.

—(1989a) [1962], *The Structural Transformation of the Public Sphere: An Inquiry into a Category of Bourgeois Society*, trans. T. Burger. Cambridge: Polity Press.

—(1989b) [1987], *The New Conservatism: Cultural Criticism and the Historians' Debate*, ed. and trans. S. Weber Nicholson. Cambridge, MA: MIT Press.

—(1990) [1983], *Moral Consciousness and Communicative Action*, trans. C. Lenhardt and S. Weber Nicholson. Cambridge: Polity Press.

—(1991) [1990], 'What Does Socialism Mean Today? The Rectifying Revolution and the Need for New Thinking on the Left', in R. Blackburn (ed.), *After the Fall: The Failure of Communism and the Future of Socialism*. London: Verso. Reprint from *New Left Review*, 183, (September/October), 1990.

—(1992a) [1990], 'Further Reflections on the Public Sphere', trans. T. Burger, in C. Calhoun (ed.), *Habermas and the Public Sphere*. Cambridge, MA: MIT Press, pp. 421–61.

—(1992b) [1988], *Postmetaphysical Thinking: Philosophical Essays*, trans. W. M. Hohengarten. Cambridge, MA: MIT Press.

—(1992c) [1990], 'Yet Again: German Identity – a Unified Nation of Angry DM-Burghers', in H. James and M. Stone (eds), *When the Wall Came Down*. New York: Routledge, pp. 86–102.

—(1993) [1991], *Justification and Application: Remarks on Discourse Ethics*, trans. C. Cronin. Cambridge: Polity Press.

—(1994) [1991], *The Past as Future*, trans. M. Pensky. Lincoln: University of Nebraska Press.

—(1996a) [1992], *Between Facts and Norms: Contributions to a Discourse Theory of Law and Democracy*, trans. W. Rehg. Cambridge: Polity Press.

—(1996b), 'Reply to Symposium Participants', *Cardozo Law Review*, 17, (nos. 4–5), 1477–557. Reprinted in M. Rosenfeld and A. Arato (eds) (1998), *Habermas on Law and Democracy: Critical Exchanges*. Berkeley: University of California Press, pp. 381–451.

—(1997) [1995], *A Berlin Republic: Writings on Germany*, trans. S. Rendall. Lincoln: University of Nebraska Press.

—(1998a), *On the Pragmatics of Communication*, ed. and trans. Maeve Cooke. Cambridge: Polity Press.

—(1998b) [1996], *The Inclusion of the Other: Studies in Political Theory*, trans. C. Cronin. Cambridge: Polity Press.

—(1999), 'Zweifellos: Eine Antwort auf Peter Handke', *Süddeutsche Zeitung*, 112, 18 May, 17.

—(2001a) [1984], *On the Pragmatics of Social Interaction: Preliminary Studies in the Theory of Communicative Action*, trans. B. Fultner. Cambridge: Polity Press.

—(2001b) [1998], *The Postnational Constellation: Political Essays*, trans. M. Pensky. Cambridge: Polity Press.

—(2001c), 'From Kant's "Ideas" of Pure Reason to the "Idealizing" Presuppositions of Communicative Action: Reflections on the Detranscendentalized "Use of Reason"', trans. B. Fultner, in W. Rehg and J. Bohman (eds), *Pluralism and the Pragmatic Turn: The Transformation of Critical Theory. Essays in Honor of Thomas McCarthy*. Cambridge, MA: MIT Press, pp. 11–39.

—(2002), *Religion and Rationality: Essays on Reason, God, and Modernity*, ed. E. Mendieta. Cambridge: Polity Press.

—(2003a) [1999], *Truth and Justification*, trans. B. Fultner. Cambridge: Polity Press.

—(2003b) [2001], *The Future of Human Nature*, trans. W. Rehg, H. Beister and M. Pensky. Cambridge, Polity Press.

—(2003c), 'Intolerance and Discrimination', *International Journal of Constitutional Law*, 1, (no. 1), 2–12.

—(2004), 'The Moral and the Ethical: A Reconsideration of the Issue of the Priority of the Right Over the Good', trans. W. Rehg, in S. Benhabib and N. Fraser (eds), *Pragmatism, Critique, Judgment: Essays for Richard J. Bernstein*. Cambridge, MA: MIT Press, pp. 29–43.

—(2006a) [2001], *Time of Transitions*, trans. C. Cronin and M. Pensky. Cambridge: Polity Press.

—(2006b) [2004], *The Divided West*, trans. C. Cronin. Cambridge: Polity Press.

—(2008) [2005], *Between Religion and Naturalism: Philosophical Essays*. Cambridge: Polity Press.

—(2009) [2008], *Europe: The Faltering Project*. Cambridge: Polity Press.

Habermas, J., von Friedeburg, L, Oehler, C. and Weltz, F. (eds) (1961), *Student und Politik: Eine Soziologische Untersuchung zum politischen Bewußtsein Frankfurter Studenten*. Neuwied: Hermann Luchterhand.

Habermas, J. and Ratzinger, J. (2005) [2005], *The Dialectics of Secularization: On Reason and Religion*, trans. B. McNeil. San Francisco: Ignatius Press.

Hegel, G. W. F. (1977) [1807], *Phenomenology of Spirit*, trans. A. V. Miller. Oxford: Oxford University Press.

Held, D. (2006), *Models of Democracy* (3rd edn). Cambridge: Polity Press.

Holub, R. C. (1991), *Jürgen Habermas: Critic in the Public Sphere*. London: Routledge.

Honig, B. (2006), 'Dead Rights, Live Futures: On Habermas's Attempt to Reconcile Constitutional Democracy', in L. Thomassen (ed.), *The Derrida-Habermas Reader*. Edinburgh: Edinburgh University Press, pp. 161–75.

Honneth, A. (1991) [1985], *The Critique of Power*, trans. K. Baynes. Cambridge, MA: MIT Press.

—(1999), 'The Social Dynamics of Disrespect: Situating Critical Theory Today', trans. J. Farrell, in P. Dews (ed.), *Habermas: A Critical Reader*. Oxford: Blackwell, pp. 320–37. Reprint from *Constellations*, 1, (no. 2), 1994, 255–69.

—(2001), 'Paradoxes of Capitalist Modernization: The Foundations of a Comprehensive Research Project of the Institute for Social Research', Institute for Social Research , Frankfurt, at http://www.ifs.uni-frankfurt. de/english/paradox.htm.

Honneth, A. and Joas, H. (eds) (1991) [1986], *Communicative Action: Essays on Jürgen Habermas's* The Theory of Communicative Action. Cambridge, MA: MIT Press.

Honneth, A., McCarthy, T., Offe, C. and Wellmer, A. (eds) (1992), *Philosophical Investigations in the Unfinished Project of Enlightenment*, trans. W. Rehg. Cambridge, MA: MIT Press.

Horkheimer, M. (1986) [1937], 'Traditional and Critical Theory', in *Critical Theory: Selected Essays*, trans. M. J. O'Connell. New York: Continuum, pp. 188–243.

—(1993) [1931], 'The Present Situation of Social Philosophy and the Tasks of the Institute for Social Research', in *Between Philosophy and Social Science. Selected Early Writings,* trans. J. Torpey. Cambridge, MA: MIT Press, pp. 1–14.

Horkheimer, M. and Adorno, T. (2002) [1947], *Dialectic of Enlightenment,* trans. E. Jephcott. Stanford: Stanford University Press.

Horster, D. and van Reijen, W. (1992), 'Interview with Jürgen Habermas', in D. Horster, *Habermas: An Introduction,* trans. H. Thompson. Philadelphia: Pennbridge, pp. 77–100.

Ingram, D. (1987), *Habermas and the Dialectic of Reason.* New Haven: Yale University Press.

Jay, M. (1973), *The Dialectical Imagination: A History of the Frankfurt School and the Institute of Social Research, 1923–1950.* Boston: Little, Brown & Co.

Kant, I. (1991a) [1784], 'An Answer to the Question: "What is Enlightenment?"', in *Political Writings,* trans. H. B. Nisbet, ed. Hans Reiss (2nd edn). Cambridge: Cambridge University Press, pp. 54–60.

—(1991b) [1795], 'Perpetual Peace: A Philosophical Sketch', in *Political Writings,* trans. H. B. Nisbet, ed. Hans Reiss (2nd edn). Cambridge: Cambridge University Press, pp. 93–130.

Kelly, M. (ed.) (1994), *Critique and Power: Recasting the Foucault/Habermas Debate.* Cambridge, MA: MIT Press.

Kohlberg, L. (1981), *Essays on Moral Development.* San Francisco: Harper & Row.

Kortian, G. (1980), *Metacritique: The Philosophical Argument of Jürgen Habermas,* trans. J. Raffan. Cambridge: Cambridge University Press.

Landes, J. B. (1992), 'Jürgen Habermas, the Structural Transformation of the Public Sphere: A Feminist inquiry', *Praxis International,* 12, (no. 1), 106–27.

Levy, D., Pensky, M. and Torpey, J. (eds) (2005), *Old Europe, New Europe, Core Europe: Transatlantic Relations After the Iraq War.* London: Verso.

Lyotard, J.-F. (1984) [1979], *The Postmodern Condition: A Report on Knowledge,* trans. G. Bennington and B. Massumi. Minneapolis: University of Minnesota Press.

MacIntyre, A. (1985), *After Virtue: A Study in Moral Theory* (2nd edn). London: Duckworth.

Marx, K. (1978) [1859], 'Preface to *A Contribution to the Critique of Political Economy*', in R. C. Tucker (ed.), *The Marx-Engels Reader* (2nd edn). New York: W. W. Norton, pp. 3–6.

Matuštík, M. B. (2001), *Jürgen Habermas: A Philosophical–Political Profile.* Lanham: Rowman & Littlefield.

Maus, I. (2002), 'Liberties and Popular Sovereignty: On Habermas's Reconstruction of the System of Rights', in R. von Schomberg and K. Baynes (eds), *Discourse and Democracy: Essays on Habermas's Between Facts and Norms.* Albany: State University of New York Press, pp. 89–128. Previously published in *Cardozo Law Review,* 17 (nos. 4–5), 1996, 825–82.

McCarthy, T. (1978), *The Critical Theory of Jürgen Habermas.* London: Hutchinson.

—(1985), 'Complexity and Democracy, or the Seducements of Systems Theory', *New German Critique*, 35, (Spring/Summer), 27–53. Reprinted in A. Honneth and H. Joas (eds) (1991) [1986], *Communicative Action: Essays on Jürgen Habermas's* The Theory of Communicative Action. Cambridge, MA: MIT Press, pp. 119–39.

—(1994), 'Kantian Constructivism and Reconstructivism', *Ethics*, 105, (no. 1), 44–63.

Mendieta, E. (2002), 'Habermas on Cloning: The Debate on the Future of the Species', *Philosophy and Social Criticism*, 30, (nos. 5–6), 721–43.

Michelman, F. I. (1999), 'Morality, Identity and "Constitutional Patriotism"', *Denver University Law Review*, 76, 1009–28.

Mouffe, C. (2000), *The Democratic Paradox*. London: Verso.

—(2005), 'For an Agonistic Public Sphere', in L. Tønder and L. Thomassen (eds), *Radical Democracy: Politics Between Abundance and Lack*. Manchester: Manchester University Press, pp. 123–32.

Müller, J. W. (2000), *Another Country: German Intellectuals, Unification and National Identity*. New Haven: Yale University Press.

Negt, O. and Kluge, A. (1993) [1972], *The Public Sphere and Experience: Toward an Analysis of the Bourgeois and Proletarian Public Sphere*, trans. P. Labanyi, J. Owen Daniel and A. Oksiloff. Minneapolis: University of Minnesota Press.

New German Critique (1985), Special Issue on Jürgen Habermas. 35 (Spring/Summer).

Norval, A. (2007), *Aversive Democracy: Inheritance and Originality in the Democratic Tradition*. Cambridge: Cambridge University Press.

Outhwaite, W. (1996), *The Habermas Reader*. Cambridge: Polity Press.

Pateman, C. (1988), 'The Fraternal Social Contract', in J. Keane (ed.), *Civil Society and the State: New European Perspectives*. London: Verso, pp. 101–28.

Pensky, M. (1998), 'Third Generation Critical Theory', in S. Critchely and W. R. Schroeder (eds), *A Companion to Continental Philosophy*. Oxford: Blackwell, pp. 407–13.

Rasmussen, D. (1990), *Reading Habermas*. Oxford: Blackwell.

Rasmussen, D. and Swindal, J. (2002a), *Jürgen Habermas. Volume I*. London: Sage.

—(2002b), *Jürgen Habermas. Volume II*. London: Sage.

—(2002c), *Jürgen Habermas. Volume III*. London: Sage.

—(2002d), *Jürgen Habermas. Volume IV*. London: Sage.

Rawls, J. (1971), *A Theory of Justice*. Cambridge, MA: Belknap Press.

—(1995), 'Reply to Habermas', *The Journal of Philosophy*, 92, (3), 132–80. Also in Rawls, J. (1996), *Political Liberalism* (2nd edn). New York: Columbia University Press, pp. 372–434.

Rehg, W. (1997), *Insight and Solidarity: The Discourse Ethics of Jürgen Habermas*. Berkeley: University of California Press.

Rosenfeld, M. and Arato, A. (eds) (1998), *Habermas on Law and Democracy: Critical Exchanges*. Berkeley: University of California Press. Previously published in *Cardozo Law Review*, 17 (nos. 4–5), 1996.

Scheuerman, W. E. (1999), 'Between Radicalism and Resignation: Democratic Theory in Habermas's *Between Facts and Norms*', in P. Dews (ed.), *Habermas: A Critical Reader*. Oxford: Blackwell, pp. 153–77. Also in von Schomberg, R. and Baynes, K. (eds) (2002), *Discourse and Democracy: Essays on Habermas's* Between Facts and Norms. Albany: State University of New York Press, pp. 61–85.

Schmitt, C. (1996) [1932], *The Concept of the Political*, trans. G. Schwab. Chicago: University of Chicago Press.

von Schomberg, R. and Baynes, K. (eds) (2002), *Discourse and Democracy: Essays on Habermas's* Between Facts and Norms. Albany: State University of New York Press.

Searle, J. (1969), *Speech Acts: An Essay in the Philosophy of Language*. Cambridge: Cambridge University Press.

Shabani, O. A. P. (2003), *Democracy, Power, and Legitimacy: The Critical Theory of Jürgen Habermas*. Toronto: University of Toronto Press.

Shaw, B. J. (1999), 'Habermas and Religious Inclusion: Lessons from Kant's Moral Theology', *Political Theory*, 27, (no. 5), 634–66.

Smith, W. (2008), 'Civil Disobedience and Social Power: Reflections on Habermas', *Contemporary Political Theory*, 7, (no. 1), 72–89.

Taylor, C. (1994), 'The Politics of Recognition', in A. Gutmann (ed.), *Multiculturalism: Examining the Politics of Recognition* (2nd edn). Princeton: Princeton University Press, pp. 25–73.

Thomassen, L. (ed.) (2006), *The Derrida-Habermas Reader*. Edinburgh: Edinburgh University Press.

—(2007), *Deconstructing Habermas*. London: Routledge.

Thompson, J. B. and Held, D. (eds) (1982), *Habermas: Critical Debates*. London: Macmillan.

Wellmer, A. (1998) [1993], *Endgames: Essays and Lectures on the Irreconcilable Nature of Modernity*, trans. D. Midgley. Cambridge, MA: MIT Press.

White, S. K. (1989), *The Recent Work of Jürgen Habermas: Reason, Justice and Modernity*. Cambridge: Cambridge University Press.

—(ed.) (1995), *The Cambridge Companion to Habermas*. Cambridge: Cambridge University Press.

Wittgenstein, L. (1958) [1953], *Philosophical Investigations*, trans. G. E. M. Anscombe (2nd edn). Oxford: Blackwell.

Wollstonecraft, M. (2004) [1792], *A Vindication of the Rights of Woman* (revised edn). London: Penguin.

Young, I. M. (1986), 'Impartiality and the Civic Public: Some Implications of Feminist Critiques of Moral and Political Theory', *Praxis International*, 5, (no. 4). Reprinted in S. Benhabib and D. Cornell (eds) (1987), *Feminism and Critique: Essays on the Politics of Gender in Late-Capitalist Societies*. Cambridge: Polity, pp. 56–76; and revised in Young, I. M. (1990), *Justice an the Politics of Difference*. Princeton: Princeton University Press, chapter 4.

—(1990), *Justice and the Politics of Difference*. Princeton: Princeton University Press.

—(1996), 'Communication and the Other: Beyond Deliberative Democracy', in S. Benhabib (ed.), *Democracy and Difference: Contesting the Boundaries of the Political*. Princeton: Princeton University Press, pp. 120–35.

—(2000), *Inclusion and Democracy*. Oxford: Oxford University Press.

—(2001), 'Activist Challenges to Deliberative Democracy', *Political Theory*, 29, (no. 5), 670–90.

Žižek, S. (2000), 'Holding the Place', in J. Butler, E. Laclau and S. Žižek, *Contingency, Hegemony, Universality: Contemporary Dialogues on the Left*. London: Verso, pp. 308–29.

INDEX

182
QM LIBRARY
(MILE END)